The Terrible & Wonderful, Ugly & Beautiful Story of My Life So Far

The Terrible & Wonderfu

gly & Beautiful
Story of My Life So Far

BY

JENNY SKYLARK KUVIN, J.D.

WITH

DONNA MADDOCK-COWART

WRITER'S PROOF

Published by Writer's Proof, an imprint of Interview You, LLC
Athens, Georgia
www.interviewyou.net

Cover and text design
by The Adsmith
www.theadsmith.com

Front cover photo: Jenny, 1979

This book is non-fiction; some names have been changed in order to protect the privacy of certain individuals.

ISBN 0-9773365-8-1
Printed in the United States of America

For Spencer, my duckbill platypus

He found him in a desert region,
In an empty howling waste.
He engirded him, watched over him,
Guarded him as the pupil of His eye.
Like an eagle who rouses his nestlings,
Gliding down to his young,
So did he spread his wings and take him,
Bear him along on His pinions;
The Lord alone did guide him,
No alien god at his side.

He set him atop the highlands,
To feast on the yield of the earth;
He fed them honey from the crag,
And oil from flinty rock…."

Deuteronomy 32:10

PREFACE

THIS IS MY STORY. Parts of it were lost to me for a long time, but when I was ready to remember, ready to begin to cope with what remembering would mean, my story came back to me.

What you will read at the beginning is what happened to me as a child and then was, mercifully, hidden from me. Then you will read of my troubled and complicated adolescence and young adulthood. This is followed by the crumbling of the fortress my consciousness had built to protect me. Then I was able to dismantle the protection from the horrible truth, and to remember, examine, and heal from that pain, to catch hold of the blessings in my world, to learn to live, to forgive what I could not understand, to build a new and beautiful life from the ashes of the old, to honor the goodness of life, to trust, and to love.

I offer my story because I was led to write it. In the writing, it became a part of my healing and thus is an aspect of my newly discovered, healing self. I was aware, too, throughout the physical and emotional work of bringing forth this book, deeply painful at times, thrillingly rewarding at others, that there is someone, somewhere, who will find comfort or strength from my story. That awareness helped give me the courage to continue, to bring to you this piece of my heart.

CHAPTER 1

The synagogue Temple Israel had two sanctuaries. The large sanctuary was huge with tall stained-glass windows on each side. The small sanctuary was plain with simple wooden pews. There were services for the children downstairs, in the recreation area. I remember walking proudly into the temple on Rosh HaShana, holding Daddy's hand. "*L Shana Tova Tika Tayvu*," ("Happy and Sweet New Year") I said to people as we passed by them.

Daddy was six feet, two inches tall and was very handsome. (He played basketball on his high school team and played state championships in the Boston Garden, where the Celtics played.)

One early memory is of a time when I wore black-patent-leather Mary Jane's over white tights with the brand new navy-and-white floral dress my mother got for me. I loved it because of the tiny navy-blue flowers that covered it, the full balloon sleeves, and the velvet bow resting in the center of my chest. It was very important to look very nice at temple, to wear just the right tights and hat.

We walked toward the large sanctuary where all my grandparents worshipped. I knew that Nana and Papa, Mommy's parents, would be in the front row. From there, I could see the beautiful silver and embroidered cases that covered the Torah up near the Ark.

I always ran to give Nana and Papa a big hug. During the service I can remember playing with the tassels on Papa's tallit, his prayer shawl, and watching the men singing. I remember Papa in a dark navy suit and vest. He had black curly hair and a mustache, beady eyes, a pointy hooked nose, and a thin-lipped smile. I thought he looked like the count from Sesame Street. Nana was four feet, eleven inches tall, and I remember looking forward to someday being taller than she was. She had short red hair and a round face and smiled often, somewhat self-consciously because of a slight gap between her front teeth. I remember her in a rust-colored wool suit, a high-necked blouse, a doily on her head, and a big diamond ring on her finger.

I always tried very hard to read the Hebrew letters in the book the men were holding. When the congregation would stand, I would run to the back where Daddy was sitting with his mother—I called her Grandma—and her sister-in-law Aunt Doris and her daughter, my cousin Dinah. Grandma was tall and broad. She wore stockings and beige shoes that looked to me like nurse's shoes. She often wore a black pillbox hat, a garnet butterfly ring, and a large smoky topaz necklace she got in Israel. She had a smaller wedding ring than Nana had.

My favorite time in the service was when the men would lift the Torah and walk around the sanctuary so everyone could touch it. They sang as they walked. The men would kiss their tallits and the Torah; the women would kiss their prayer books and touch the Torah. Papa was in the front row, and he raised me up way high and gave me his prayer book so I could kiss it and touch the Torah for good luck.

On December 29, 1970, I was born at 10:10 a.m. at Beth Israel Hospital in Boston, Massachusetts. I was born with forceps-indent marks on either side of my head and later was told that I was ugly then, but that Nana said I would get better. That day, so the story was told, Papa broke into the hospital room with a cheer and a fur coat; he threw the coat at my mother, his daughter, and said, "Now we are even." In spite of the forceps marks, he always thought I was beautiful. I was his favorite.

My parents—in their twenties when I was born, very successful—moved from a small apartment to a duplex in Randolph, Massachusetts, and my grandparents visited us every day. Then my parents sold the duplex after my sister was born and we moved to a house in Sharon, an upper-middle-class, half-Jewish, half-Catholic suburb of Boston, the same suburb they had grown up in. (My parents were high-school sweethearts.) My three surviving grandparents lived very close to us. My grandparents still came over every day; they would come over and have dinner and visit us. I would sit on Papa's lap and look into the paper bag he held; he would have presents for me every day.

I was two and a half when Allison was born. She became

Nana's favorite, and I remained Papa's favorite. We lived what probably seemed to the outside world a normal life, a good life. My grandparents had an expensive house in Cape Cod, and a big house in Sharon. Papa owned a chain of jewelry stores. We were a very successful family.

Sharon, Massachusetts, where we all lived for most of my childhood, is a small New England town. My mother and father and Allison and I had our house. Grandma lived one mile away, and Nana and Papa lived two miles away. The town had its own dairy, and the milkman delivered fresh milk and orange juice in glass bottles every week.

The rhythm of our days was regular and comforting. The beginning of evening was marked by Daddy's arrival home. Often Allison and I were outside riding bikes in the neighborhood when Mom called us in for dinner. I had what I considered then an awesome banana-seat bike (the seat was covered in denim), and Allison rode her big wheels. Allison and I got along pretty well. We played spin art together and other games. We really liked to play together, but sometimes I could get a little bossy. As long as Allison was listening to me, I would play with her. As soon as she wanted to go her own way, I would get frustrated. I could stay in my room for hours, drawing, dancing, reading. Sometimes I liked to play choreographer and direct Allison and maybe one of her friends in a dance. Early on, I didn't have my own friends; my mother didn't like that.

Every night Mom made a complete dinner. My favorite was lamb chops, mashed potatoes, and corn. There was always a salad before dinner and a dessert at the end, often one of Nana's brownies.

Certain days were marked by regular events. On Tuesdays I knew I had to finish my reading and practice clarinet before eight o'clock because Fonzi was on. My sister and I loved Fonzi. "Happy Days," we thought, was the best program on TV. On Tuesdays, also, we had hopes that Mom would let us stay up to watch "Laverne and Shirley."

Typically at dinner, Allison and I told Daddy about our day. Sometimes there was something special arranged; for instance, one time we really wanted to show Daddy our new dance routine, and Nana and Papa had been invited for the performance. After dinner, Daddy and Mommy and Nana and Papa sat in the living room, and Allison and I gave a good show. Then Nana and Papa went home, and Daddy gave the happy dancers a bath. After bath time, I put on my favorite nightgown and helped Allison with hers. Then the family gathered in the TV room in the basement to watch "Happy Days."

Every day Mommy packed the same brown-bag lunch for me. The sandwich was always one of these three: kosher salami, tuna fish, or peanut butter and jelly. It came with either chips or Fritos. I also had a Ring Ding, Devil Dog, or Twinkie and always a piece of fruit, whatever was in season or fresh at the time—an apple, orange, pear, peach, or plum.

Lunch time and recess were back-to-back in grade school, and I would buy my milk from the cafeteria and take my lunch outside to the playground. A lot of times the girls were playing jacks. We also jumped rope.

The only thing more fun than recess at school, especially in winter, was no school at all: a snow day. When the snow would fall, Allison and I would sit in front of the TV and watch the names of the elementary schools go by and pray that we would have the day off. If a lot of snow fell and the trucks with salt for the roads were running late, the buses wouldn't run. We were so excited when we saw the name of our school on the list. No school meant hours outside making snow angels and snow men.

My dance class was important to me, and, of course, the recitals were important family events. Children's dance recitals can last for up to three hours. It could be torturous for most adults, but the parents were excited and proud to see their children perform.

When we would be driving places in the car, there was always music. Mommy loved Grace Jones, Patty Labelle, and Bette Midler. Daddy loved Neil Diamond. And everyone loved Barry Manilow, Harry Chapin, and Meatloaf. I remember Mommy and Daddy singing both parts of "Paradise by the Dashboard Light" on many road trips.

As I got a bit older, making friends in suburbia became easier for me because the kids available were either my mother's friends' kids or the other kids in our neighborhood, and most of them were boys or girls younger than me. My best friend was a boy named Jeremy. Except for him, I was older than all the kids around our block. Unfortunately, this meant when Mommy and Daddy couldn't find a babysitter and needed me to have a sleepover, this didn't leave many choices. Sometimes I slept at Nana and Papa's house.

I remember one year when I was really excited about my birthday party. It was going to be at a pizza place, Papa Gino's, and I was going to be able to make my own pizza. Papa Gino's was in the next town over, where all the cool things were. Next to Papa Gino's was a penny-candy store where I loved getting red-cinnamon silver dollars. Across the street was Friendly's, where I always got a strawberry fribble milkshake. Down the street were Bradlees and the new discount clothing store called Marshall's. Right around the corner from that was the Candle Pin Bowling Alley. Mommy was really good at bowling. She played in a league.

Watching Mommy get ready to go out on Friday nights was good and bad. It was good because I loved watching Mommy put on her makeup and pick out her clothes. Mommy had beautiful olive skin, not freckled like mine. Her hair was thick, jet-black, and curly, not thin and brown like mine. Mommy was really beautiful. She didn't seem to think so, though. She always asked me if she looked okay or if she looked too fat.

The bad part about Friday nights watching Mommy get

ready was I knew that Mommy and Daddy were going to leave. Allison and I hated that they left. Often we cried. It wasn't so bad when we had a cool babysitter like Sherry, a girl we both liked very much. Also, maybe Donny and Marie would be on TV.

Allison and I loved Donny and Marie. My favorite color was purple, just like Donny's. I would spend hours looking in the mirror and singing and dancing like Marie. I would practice smiling and making faces. My fine, straight dark-brown hair was in a sort of long Dorothy Hamill cut. I had dark-brown almond-shaped eyes, a button nose, and just a sprinkle of freckles on each cheek. I was very thin from all my dancing and had long legs.

Mommy was always doing something, and I was just like her, always busy. She was either needle pointing, doing macramé, knitting, crocheting, or weaving. And when she wasn't doing needlework, she was playing mahjong or bowling in the bowling league.

Mommy was also involved in ORT, a Jewish women's service organization, with our neighbor Roberta Weinstein. Roberta had a daughter, Jaime, who was close to my age. I couldn't stand her. She always had boogers in her nose and looked like a slob. Her house was always messy. They had hamsters in the basement, and the hamsters caused a big mess all over. Their house smelled bad, too. Roberta always seemed to be wearing her nightgown.

Roberta's husband, Jeff, was just as gross. He gave me dirty looks and then laughed. He often would walk around with his belly hanging out, and he had an ugly little tattoo of a devil. I remember him laughing and calling it the "horny little devil." One day I was walking home from their house, and Jeff grabbed me and put his hand up my skirt. "Now, don't tell your daddy," he said. I didn't, but I did try to tell my parents that I thought the Weinsteins were gross. "Gross" was the only word I could find for this. Daddy just said, "Don't be silly. They are our friends."

"But I hate them, Daddy!"

"That's not nice," he replied. "You shouldn't hate people."

One time I was supposed to stay the night with them when Mom and Dad were away. My parents took me there, but I didn't stay. I ran away to Grandma's house. I just left and walked down the street to Grandma's house, and my parents let me stay there instead.

CHAPTER 2

When I stayed with Nana and Papa, many times they had some friends over, and I was told to play by myself. That was when I started playing the face game. I learned to see faces in anything around the house. Sometimes I would talk to them and sometimes not: they weren't really there. I knew that. But the toys at Nana and Papa's house were old and boring, so the faces kept me company. I could see really good faces in wood paneling. Nana kept dried flowers around her house; she rarely had fresh flowers. In a few rooms there were pussy-willow branches, pointy sticks with little fuzzy things at intervals on them. I would break them off and tickle my nose with them.

Nana was not supposed to drink alcohol; it made her crazy. Everyone said she was allergic to it. When I was at her house Nana was always teaching me what seemed to be all the important things. She taught me how to clean and how to fold laundry. There was a big linen closet for the sheets and towels at the top of the staircase leading to the bedrooms. Nana hid her bottle of alcohol in the laundry basket she kept on the bottom shelf. This was our secret.

At one point, Mommy and Daddy became disco maniacs. They both let their thick, curly hair go wild so they had Afros. They learned a dance called the "Hustle." At night Allison and I loved watching them dance around to Donna Summer.

My hair was straight. At one point Mommy thought it might look neat with a perm. It was awful. I hated it.

One Saturday we had a different babysitter, the boy who lived next door. He seemed nice enough. However, as the night went on, he wanted Allison and me to play games. At first we played the pop-up game Trouble, and then he wanted to play a different game. In this game, Allison and I had to take turns letting him touch us between our legs. He asked us to lie with him on the couch. It was weird.

Some weekends I was lucky enough to stay with Grandma, Daddy's mom. Her house was much quieter than ours. Grandma played Monopoly and Rummy Q with me. She also let me lie in her lap while she played with my hair. At Grandma's, I could rest. It was peaceful there.

Grandma was very different from Nana. She couldn't make a brisket like Nana's, and she was very independent. Whereas Nana barely drove, Grandma jetted around town easily in her tan Chevette. Grandma was poor compared to Nana and Papa. Daddy's father had died when he was young, so Grandma had to finish raising her three sons alone. To make ends meet, she taught Hebrew school; she also did electrolysis in an office in the basement. There she had a doctor's chair and a mirror and tools for when the women would come over for treatment. Because Grandma was busy, her house hadn't changed from when Daddy was young. The kitchen still had pink linoleum, and the bathroom had a crocheted doll to cover the toilet paper roll. Even the bedroom that Daddy and his brother, Uncle Ronald, had shared still had their bunk beds in it.

Uncle Ronald had lived with Grandma ever since the Vietnam War. He was a really good auto mechanic and piano player. He was schizophrenic and sometimes fought with Grandma. Mommy told me that before the Vietnam War, Uncle Ronald was normal and was more handsome than Elvis.

On Sundays we all had breakfast together. Mom made salami and eggs or fried matzo. If Nana and Papa were with us, the conversation always turned to Israel and what was going on there. Ensuring the survival of the State of Israel was very important to everyone. Since the Seven Day War and the assassinations in Munich, this had seemed even more urgent than usual. Every year on Tubeshvat the children of the temple collected money to plant trees in Israel. And every house had a small metal blue-and-white Tzedakah box for charity to be sent to Israel. Every year for my birthday I received an Israeli bond.

Papa, my grandfather, often made plans for my future. One week Papa thought I should be a doctor; he brought me a book starring Mr. Goodbody, a freak wearing a unitard with body parts painted on it. It was supposed to teach me about anatomy. I didn't want to read it. I wanted to read *Nancy Drew*, the *Hardy Boys*, or my *Little House* series. I really didn't want to be a doctor. I thought I might like to be a dancer.

We spent parts of every summer in Cape Cod at Nana and Papa's house. It was a large Cape-Cod style home with a big wraparound porch. The floors inside were wood, covered with large, braided-wool rugs. Mom and Allison and Nana and I would be there all week, and Papa and Daddy would come out on the weekends. During the day I would plant and then tend tomatoes in Nana's garden and go digging for clams on the beach. Every morning on the Cape, Mommy, Allison, and I took our beach chairs and walked down to the ocean. Nana would pack fruit and sandwiches. We would stay as long as our faces didn't get too red. We would always wait for the ice-cream man to come. I would have an orange sherbet push-up, Allison would have a rocket pop, Nana would have a strawberry shortcake bar, and Mommy would have a banana Popsicle.

Nana called every single one of my freckles "angel kisses" and named them until there were too many to name. When we would get home from the beach, Allison and I would take showers, and Nana would rub lotion and powder on our red bodies. Allison and I shared a bedroom upstairs with two twin beds, and every night Nana would sing us to sleep.

There was a green hammock on the porch. When my grandparents' friend Hal and his wife would come for the weekend, Hal would sit and swing on the hammock. I couldn't stand him; he scared me. He always kissed me with wet kisses, and he always pinched me. When they were there, I spent as much time as I could hiding on the back porch, picking the white paint off the porch rails.

Papa made his money with a chain of jewelry stores in Boston. He had a rule about my getting my ears pierced. I could get them pierced, but not until I was at least five years old. The summer when I was five, Papa arrived one weekend, and we all knew he was going to pierce my ears. He sat me on a stool in the kitchen, the entire family watching. He marked both ears with a pen. I felt a pinch, and the left ear was pierced. The right ear was marked, but, unfortunately, Papa missed the mark. He told me it would be okay; he would be able to pierce the right ear again as soon as the hole closed up.

Soon after that, my sister and I started going to camp for part of the summer. One summer all the kids went to Sharon Country Day Camp. Every morning Mommy would get up and give Allison and me breakfast and pack our lunches and camp duffle bags, and then we went out to the bus stop. We were stars at camp. It was fun for me because I was good at almost every activity. Allison and I both won best camper that summer. That summer at camp I also met my first real best friend. This was awesome because my new friend was going to be at the new school I was starting the next school year.

The basement of our house was so cool. Daddy had wood-paneled the entire thing and built a bar and a platform for our new pinball machine. He also built a playroom for our toys. My friends and I spent hours downstairs playing. The TV was down there, and that's where our family relaxed together.

When Mom got pregnant with my little brother, my parents put an addition on the house. My room was redone, and I thought it was magnificent. I had navy-blue-and-white shag carpet with navy-blue wallpaper printed with big, bright red, yellow, and green tulips. I had twin beds for sleepovers and a beautiful dresser and desk.

I also had a new music stand to hold my music for my clarinet. I loved playing the clarinet and was really getting good at it.

It was around this time that I began to realize that I couldn't play anymore with the neighborhood boys the way I always had. One day they were climbing in and out of the water tunnel at the end of the street. Greg Stone was there with his big brother. I didn't like Greg, but he wanted me to be his girlfriend. That day his big brother and two of his friends held me down so Greg could give me a kiss.

My little brother was born, and he was the first grandson. This was so exciting. The bris, the circumcision ceremony, was celebrated in our newly renovated home. Everyone was there, including Hal, who at one point made his way back to my room to harass me for a second and pinch me. Papa and Hal had arrived late, and they were both drunk. When they arrived, they drove onto the front lawn. Mommy and Nana were furious.

When I think about that time, I remember Mommy's pretty navy blue car. She'd get her hair and nails done at the beauty parlor; she liked to buy pretty clothes for herself. Nana, on the other hand, was scared to drive. She sometimes drove around town in the little brown Pinto Papa bought her. But she preferred that Papa drive her. She dyed her own hair and knit her own sweaters. She hardly ever bought anything for herself without Papa's permission. She shaved her legs without using water. It looked like it hurt. Nana just didn't do nice things for herself.

When Daddy's construction business was booming, Mommy wanted to build a bigger home. She and Daddy picked out a lot and designed what would be the biggest house in town at the time, over 4,000 square feet. It had one central great room and four wings, each pyramid shaped and connected by hallways. The dining room and the living room, with white carpet and a huge fireplace and the piano, were in one wing. In another wing were all three children's bedrooms and a spiral staircase leading up to the playroom loft. In another wing was the master suite with his-and-her dressing rooms, a Jacuzzi tub, and two showers. In the final wing was the garage with a staircase leading to a loft, which was Daddy's office. In the center great room was the second fireplace, decorated with a beautiful loom-woven work of art my mother had made. In front of the fireplace was a black-with-tan-pinstripes sectional sofa facing the TV, which was equipped with the latest Atari game, Pong. To the left of the TV were four large French doors leading to the backyard. In front of the French doors was a card table set up for mahjong games. The kitchen was on the opposite side of the great room. There were ceiling-high storage cabinets. The floors were beautiful wood grain. The window above the sink looked out onto the front circular driveway.

My room in this house was classic. It was the late seventies, and my mom picked out peach and brown for the colors. The wallpaper was a peach-rose floral on brown paper with metallic accents. The carpet was a mixed thin weave with flecks of brown and peach. My bed was an antique four poster with white lace bedding. My wooden dollhouse—Daddy built it and Mommy and I decorated it—sat on a carefully chosen antique sewing machine. The room also held my clarinet practice chair and a beautiful brass antique music stand that was a Hanukah present.

The room was magnificent: a room for a princess.

CHAPTER 3

The first time I remember it happening, it was cold out. No one would have found it remarkable that the afghan had made its way onto Papa's lap. It was a real seventies creation, crocheted by Nana in orange, yellow, pea green, and black.

I was eight years old. The Celtics were doing well again, and the entire family gathered in the den to watch the game. Most were seated on the two orange Berber couches which were placed near the wood-paneled walls. Daddy and Mommy's brother, Uncle Jeff—who had matching Afros—were on one couch. On the other sat my mother, her clanking knitting needles busy, working on a sweater for cousin Jacob's new baby, Mark. My sister, Allison, sat there, too. In the kitchen off the den, Nana was baking something yummy, probably brownies with walnuts or the rolled cinnamon cookies she called "dreidels." The clanking of the needles, the quiet sound of the rolling of the dough, and the screaming every time Bird hit a three-pointer off the Chief created an atmosphere that was only made cozier by cigarette smoke and the sound of the nutcracker cracking nuts. It was loud and busy, lots going on.

I was sitting with Papa, as usual. His chair was a very big black leather chair that had a footrest. It was where he sat to watch the TV, which was on the opposite wall. Next to the big black chair was a fireplace with a huge orange painting by my Aunt Judy, my mother's sister. Papa always put his cigarettes out in the ashtray that was shaped like a shotgun. And he always had the nuts with the nutcracker close by. I always sat on his lap every time I visited. He was my favorite person in the world. I would giggle and laugh with him. He continued to make it clear that I was his favorite.

I didn't really know what to do when I felt Papa reach down underneath the afghan and touch me. But I understood that I wasn't supposed to move. Papa was holding me tight. His hands were cold, and his fingernails were just a little too long. They hurt me just a little. I stared at my parents and the TV set. A newsbreak came on with a story about some people who were driving around playgrounds in a white van and giving drugs to children. The people in the room remarked about how awful that was. He kept rubbing, and I kept quiet. Papa was in charge. He loved me and controlled me.

I realize now but certainly could not have understood at that time that my boundaries—both physical and spiritual—did not react to him, for almost every day in my life so far he had visited me and carefully created and then violated these boundaries, first by playing exciting games on his lap. There was that paper-bag game, for instance, where he would give me a paper bag, and sometimes there was a present at the bottom of the bag and sometimes it was empty, but almost every day he would play this game with me. He bought me many presents. I sat on his lap at shows, movies, and temple. He whispered in my ear constantly. I knew that he loved me. I was certain he did.

When he started to touch me, I didn't understand what was happening, but I know that I thought these feelings were in the same realm as love. This was just between us.

After this first time, it became his custom. There we would be in a room full of people, and he would put a blanket over the two of us and touch me in a way no one else did. This was love. This was special. It was our connection. It was our secret.

CHAPTER 4

After Hanukah and before Passover was a really fun time at temple. It was on Purim that the children would dress up as each of the characters from the book of Esther and celebrate Esther saving the Jewish people. I remember dressing up as Queen Esther. Grandma picked me up, and we drove to temple for the reading of The Book of Esther. This was so much fun. During the reading, every time we heard the name of the evil guy, Haman, we would rattle the Macgregor and yell. I stayed up pretty late that night because there was a lot of dancing and eating. I slept at Grandma's house.

The first night of Passover, the holiday that celebrates the delivery of the Jews from slavery, was always held at

Nana and Papa's house. At their house, the china cabinet at one end of the dining room had china and crystal in it. Papa sat in the end chair in front of the table. The kitchen was off to the left side of Papa, so Nana sat on that side of Papa, and I always sat to his right. The head of the household always dictates the nature of the Passover Seder. Papa was very strict and organized about his. I would sing the Kiddush, the blessing over the wine. I had learned it in Hebrew School. With a wink from both Papa and Daddy, I knew I had performed well.

One celebration stands out in my memory. I remember very clearly when it was time for the four questions, which are traditionally sung in Hebrew by the youngest child. It was a year when Allison was the youngest—the year I was nine years old—and she was able to sing the questions. With every ritual in the Passover Seder, a new type of food is used. In between every portion was a blessing with both Nana and my mom rushing in and out of the kitchen. There was a small plate for the bitter herbs, the horseradish used to symbolize the mortar from the bricks of the pyramids the Jews had to build and so on. The scene is usually very noisy, a real family-holiday atmosphere. Each person at the table reads a little in Hebrew from the story of Moses and the Israelites being delivered to the Promised Land. After the story is completed, a few songs are sung, and the meal is served.

The head of the Seder is in charge of hiding the afikomen, which is a piece of matzo. And then the children look for the piece of matzo and get a silver dollar when it's found. Papa often hid the matzo underneath the table pads. No one would ever think twice when Papa reached over to whisper into my ear. I was spending the night at their house that night, and Papa was reminding me to meet him in the den later. I wouldn't dare disobey him.

You had to eat fast because Nana picked up your plate almost as fast as she gave it to you: first the gefilte fish and then the matzo ball soup, then the brisket, and chicken with green beans and potatoes.

After the meal was the most fun because we would all sing songs. My father and I would sing every single one. Papa was bored by this time, so he would go over to the living room to the drink cart and pour himself a glass of Scotch, Scotch which he shared with me later that night. The living room sofas had plastic on them, and the drapes were pea-green velvet. The wallpaper was ornate. There was a large painting done by my Aunt Judy. I thought it was strange; it was of three or four men. They looked like rabbis.

The piano was in the other room. Everyone knew how to play piano. My mother or aunt could pick up the thick "fake" book at any time and play a tune. After the meal the family had some dessert and coffee and then everyone except Allison and I would leave. We would sleep in the bedroom upstairs that my mother and aunt had slept in during high school, in their two beds. Nana was fond of fast, very hot showers, so after a very quick shower we crawled into bed, and Nana sang us to sleep. Nana also read a poem from a book of poems that Papa had given me. The poem we liked the best was one that had a line in it about "between the dark and the daylight," about two daughters and their father. Nana would also sing lots of songs.

The second night of Passover was always with Daddy's family. We went over to Daddy's oldest brother's house and had Seder with him and his wife and two daughters. This Seder was a lot more fun. All the girls would sing the entire service, including the songs at the end. Uncle Robert, a successful trial attorney, was a lot less tense than Papa with his Seder. He was also less transparent with the hiding of the matzo. He was really trying to hide it.

CHAPTER 5

One year Papa wanted me to become a politician, probably the first female Jewish president someday. He wanted me to run for treasurer of the temple youth group. I didn't want to. He insisted. He even bought the poster board for my campaign posters and made buttons with my name on them. I really didn't want to run. I wanted to sing and dance. I ran and lost.

Dancing lessons, clarinet lessons, Hebrew school, Girl Scouts, and now singing lessons. When the teacher in chorus asked for volunteers to audition for the solo in fourth grade, my friends encouraged me to try. The song was "Tomorrow" from the new musical *Annie*. I went up to the front and belted out, "The sun will come out tomorrow!"

I won the solo. And I remember coming home and kind of nonchalantly telling my mother about it. After the recital one of the local voice teachers, Miss Sally, approached my mother and asked her if she would like her to give me lessons. Miss Sally lived just down the street, so after school on Wednesdays I would walk from home to Miss Sally's house and take lessons at the piano in the basement.

In fourth grade I changed schools because we had moved into our new house. I used to perform and sing in the mirror in my room for hours. My sister and I were always dancing and playing "star."

Papa turned my beautiful voice into another way to manipulate and confuse me sexually. He told me my voice was ugly and loud and embarrassing. By this time, his touching me had escalated to the point that when I would spend the night at Papa and Nana's house, he would have me sneak to him during the night to play "games" with him when Nana was sleeping.

CHAPTER 6

Semen tastes like bleach. I knew this when I was a little girl because that is what Papa told me when he first asked me to take him in my mouth. I didn't quite understand what was happening. All I can recall is that I tried to talk to Papa. At one point it seemed like he was the only person that liked me. I thought that all my friends at school thought I was a show-off and didn't want to be my friend. I tried to tell Papa how sad I was. Nana had gone to bed, and Papa was up watching the news. He let me watch with him.

Papa quickly told me that he loved me very much. After that he asked me to touch him; he had on his pajama pants. He then went on and told me again how much he loved me. He told me that Nana said he was fat and that she didn't like him anymore. He tried to convince me to put him in my mouth. He told me that my mother's sister Judy had done this for him and that this was what I was supposed to do, too. I didn't understand what he meant. I couldn't quite understand how this was happening. I was just trying to tell him my feelings. But he didn't care. I was starting to understand that he only cared about himself.

I resisted him, and he pulled at my arm and reminded me that he was the only person who truly loved me and said if I didn't make him happy, he would not love me anymore. I grazed him with my big front teeth, and he pulled my hair.

And then it happened for the first time: I split.

Half of me went to the kitchen and the other half remained in the den. The half that remained quickly said, "Don't be such a wimp. Wait out here. I will do it." And my other half watched from outside, confused and certain that I was crazy.

The next day, Mom let me skip Hebrew school to watch Luke and Laura's wedding on General Hospital with Shari and another friend. We were making jokes about boys, pretending to know more than we did. And I blurted out, "It tastes like bleach." The two neighborhood girls looked at me. "You're weird," they said.

I watched "Days of Our Lives" with Grandma (my father's mother), "All My Children" and "Another World" with Mommy, and "General Hospital" with my friends. So, of course, when my boyfriend Andy Rosen's best friend, John Freeman, confessed his love, I was sure this was just like Roman and Marlena or Luke and Laura, in addition to feeling exhilarated and special that two boys liked me at the same time.

Nana was very superstitious. She taught me all the good superstitions, beginning with "never step under a ladder or on a crack." She also knew every person famous or not who was Jewish and thought everyone that wasn't wanted to kill us. I spent hours with Nana in the kitchen. We looked so much alike it was almost spooky. We were both left-handed. I thought our similarities were why Nana seemed to understand me so well. I knew that Nana understood my splitting because Nana split, too.

Usually everyone knew when Nana split; most of the

time, she drank before she did it. Usually she would become grossly violent and rude and either start hitting me on the head really hard with a hairbrush or kitchen utensil or she would start cleaning like a maniac. I knew not to interfere. I would say even while she was hitting me: "I know, Nana, get it out; I know, Nana, just let it out."

I think one way Nana made herself feel better about the splitting, something that helped her feel that it wasn't abnormal, was to make fun of other people who had sudden mood changes. Sometimes Nana would refer to my sister Allison as "Allison One" or "Allison Two." If Allison threw a temper tantrum, then she was the "Bad Allison," and if she was being sweet, she was the "Good Allison." I thought Nana could read my mind when she did this. I thought she was talking to me. I knew that there was no Allison One or Two, but I saw the two Nanas, and I was beginning to master the art of splitting into two as well.

CHAPTER 7

Two of my favorite holidays—Simchat Torah and Sukkos—come after the High Holy Days. On Simchat Torah, we would march in the street outside the synagogue to celebrate the Torah. On Sukkos the whole congregation helped to build a large Sukkos on the outside of the temple. This structure was a wood canopy like that which the Israelites used in the desert so long ago. We decorated the Sukkos with fruit and vegetables. We always ate one meal together outside in the Sukkos. It was a lot of fun.

Grandma took Hebrew school really seriously. While the class was in session, she didn't let me call her Grandma, and she expected more from me than from the rest of the class. I was more than happy to oblige. I loved school and loved being the teacher's pet. I also loved temple and learning to read and write Hebrew. It meant I would be able to read the book I looked at every weekend at services.

When a Brownie becomes a Girl Scout, it can be a pretty fancy ceremony. Both Mom and Dad came to watch me become a Girl Scout cadet. I walked over a symbolic bridge, and my scout leader replaced my Brownie cap with a fancy green beret symbolizing I had become a cadet. I had den meetings on Fridays and wore my Girl Scout outfit to school and then walked to the meeting after school with my friend Andrea.

I always raised my hand in class and made it obvious that I loved learning. This really annoyed Steve King, a kid who was clearly from the wrong side of the tracks. He often taunted me and called me a "brown noser, know-it-all." The school was an old building, and we kids kept our stuff in a coat closet. We each had our own hook and cubby. Steve King frequently cornered me in the coat closet and picked me up and hung me by my clothes on a hook. He said if I tried to tell on him, he would beat me up. He hated me. He hated everything about me. He hated my clothes, my money, and everything. On Fridays when I was in my Girl

Scout uniform, he was particularly cruel.

When I sang "Walking in a Winter Wonderland" and "Silver Bells" in the auditorium in front of the whole school for the winter recital, I could see Steve King watching me from the audience. He smiled in a way that let me know that I might feel great now but that later on, he'd have me hanging from a hook again.

Steve was a bad part of my daytime world; in my nighttime world, the abuse continued. I prayed for it to stop. I prayed. God did not listen.

In the better part of my daytime world, my vocal gifts brought a lot of opportunities. Miss Sally had heard of auditions in Boston for the movie version of *Annie*. Mom, Grandma, Nana, and I traveled into the city together for the auditions. I made it all the way to the final four girls. Unfortunately, it turned out that I was a bit too old because filming was not going to begin for a year. No one knew, of course, that I had made a deal with God: I'll stay alive if I can be Annie. I thought the part in the movie *Annie* was going to be my escape. When I didn't get it, I was heartbroken.

My mother responded with action: she wouldn't give up until she found something to make up for my disappointment and lost opportunity. She found a unique music camp in Maine for musically gifted children. I auditioned and was accepted. I would be the youngest camper there the following summer. I attended this music camp for two summers. I spent those summers learning musical theory and performing in many musicals and operettas. I learned scales, breath exercises, and lots of new songs.

Another plus was that due to the temporary renown brought by the audition, for a short time everyone wanted to be friends with me. So I had a big birthday party at the roller rink, followed by a sleepover.

CHAPTER 8

The path up to my cabin the first summer I went to music camp was lined with fresh blackberries. Every time I walked up the hill, I picked as many as I could. It was exciting to be the youngest camper accepted into this camp. It was very scary for the first couple of weeks, and I cried myself to sleep every night at first. The children in my cabin were not very friendly towards me. It seemed that when most children my age heard me sing, they were not friendly toward me. A few bullies in school the past year had made me aware of this fact and slightly more tolerant of the other children's treatment of me.

I had a very strong voice for a little girl my size. When I sang, it commanded the attention of everyone around. That and all of my secrets made me seem, I think now, older, different, and more mature. I suppose this is why I made friends with campers that were slightly older than me. I found myself sort of adopted by the older teenage campers. Ellen, a flute player, would let me sit in her room for hours watching her practice. Helen taught me about boys and music. She played Led Zeppelin for me. Ken, a jazz pianist, would let me sit on the piano while he played. He would talk to me for hours about jazz and music. When Mom and Dad and Nana and Papa came up for visiting day, I was set to perform as Mary Poppins. I hated the costume, a big pink hat and ugly scarf with a silly umbrella that didn't match the other pieces. Most of all I hated it because the teacher, like most grownups, did not really listen to me and was forcing me to sing in a way I hated.

I didn't want to do it. It was going to look stupid. Then Papa would be right. My voice was ugly. And he couldn't be right; I didn't want him to be right. I was confused: how could a voice be good and bad. Mom and Dad and even Ken had to convince me, had to talk me into performing that day. Papa just sat there with a look of disgust on his face, like I had dared to embarrass him and his family. He sent daggers of shame my way, and I absorbed them into my psyche with "A Spoonful of Sugar."

In day camp that summer, I didn't find things to be as easy as the first time. During the time I spent in music camp, my friends had made new friends. Although I still excelled in all the activities, I was not making friends as easily. I think the abuse, which was accelerating, and my reactions to it were causing me to act really strange at times, and I was becoming very self-conscious. My friends wanted less and less to do with me. I was angry and not much fun to be around anymore.

This year I was old enough to participate in camp sleepovers. One of the rituals we did on sleepovers was called "fire circle." To be selected for fire circle was a very important privilege, and you didn't know whether you'd been chosen until the campfire at night. The best girl athlete and best boy athlete from each age group is selected. At the campfire the chosen ones were tapped on the shoulder and then blindfolded and taken across the lake for a secret initiation. The honored ones were presented to the entire camp at the daily flagpole session the next morning. The other campers would know who had been chosen by the headdress on their heads and the Indian paint on their faces. I was selected! I was thrilled to be honored this way.

I developed a close friendship with one of my camp counselors, a girl named Elaine. One day when my mother couldn't pick me up from camp, Elaine took me home to her house. At her house Elaine showed me her cool camouflage pants and field hockey stick. She also explained to me what a lesbian is. Then she asked me to play a game. I was feeling uneasy, and I really didn't want to play the game. But I didn't want to lose my new friend. Elaine asked me to lie on the bed, and then she began to kiss me between my legs. This felt really weird and sort of good.

Then Elaine told me it was my turn and that I had to kiss her as she had kissed me. It was awful. I didn't want to do it, but Elaine said that it wasn't fair because she had just done it for me. She made me look at her, and I felt yucky. She kept insisting, though, and I began to do it. Elaine started to move. I became frightened, and I screamed, "I want to go home now." Elaine got up, and I ran to the door. We went out and got in her car. I began banging my head against the window of the car. "You're bad, bad, bad," kept going through my mind. Elaine said she was sorry.

When I got home, my mother noticed that something was wrong. She looked at me as if asking what was bothering me. "Mommy, I am gross and yucky," I said.

Mom didn't understand. All she could say was, "No, you are not. You're a beautiful little girl."

I didn't believe her.

I began to feel that I didn't want to smile. My two front teeth, I was convinced, were big and ugly. I could feel them on my front lips, and they felt awkward. That combined with the permanent my mom thought would thicken my hair made me look, I thought, like Bozo the clown. Plus Mom would only buy me the canvas Nikes and not the leather kind everyone else had.

CHAPTER 9

I was scared this time. The last time I had to meet Papa at night he had really hurt me, and I had been afraid I was going to die. I did not have anyone to talk to, so I pretended to talk to my sleeping little sister. "I love you, Allison. If he kills me, I want you to know how much I love you." I was afraid he would try to hurt Allison next because I had seen that he had already begun to hold her more and treat her in a way that made me suspicious.

I tiptoed down the stairs where he was waiting in the den. He got me a Scotch and sat with me on the orange Berber couch. He began to talk again about how sad he was that Nana didn't love him anymore and called him "fat" and that she would not satisfy him anymore. He also went on to say that he knew I loved him because I pleased him the way I did. He also went on to say how proud he was of my singing voice and how it prepared me for pleasing him.

I hoped and prayed that he would become aroused from my mouth; he hadn't last time. And if he didn't, he would get angry and sad, and he would have to try something else. What he did was to force me to lie on the couch face down, all the while repeating over and over, "You know how much Papa loves you." He would pull my hair until I said, "Yes, I know you love me."

This time I felt that I was going to die here; I was sure of it. The pain was so bad. With each penetration, the sturdy fabric of the couch rubbing on my face, I got angrier and angrier. "Yes, I know you love me. Yes, I know you love me." The repeated motion and the position I was in caused my body to respond and a sudden wave of paralyzing pleasure seized my body, taking me completely by surprise. Papa suddenly stopped, realizing what had happened. He turned me over, raised his hand, and hit me. He picked me up so he could see my face and almost spat out one word: "Whore!" He threw me to the floor.

On the floor, I felt the brown shag carpet against my

face. Dazed, I looked up at the orange-sun painting above the fireplace. I was going to die. The pain inside my back did not even come close to the shattering knife pain that ran through my chest. I knew I had to get up. If I didn't survive to do what he wanted, he would get Allison. I lay there, trying to compose myself. And I heard a voice from inside myself. It was a kind voice. "Don't worry, Jennifer," it said. "The pain you are in now is equal to the love you will feel later." The quality and kindness of the voice and what was said comforted me. I pulled on my clothes and went up to bed.

CHAPTER 10

It seems to me now that suburbia in the late seventies was all about being spoiled and stoned. All the parents were young and rich. One year Mom and Dad threw a New Year's Eve party, a costume party. We kids slept over at Nana's, so I don't know what happened that night, but I did hear my Mom talking about someone's mom caught in the hot tub with someone else's dad. I also found little glass vials of white powder in my Mom's bathroom.

Rena and Michael Stone and my parents went to school together and our two families were very good friends. Every year we celebrated at least one of the eight nights of Hanukah together. This year it was the fifth night. I quickly opened up my present and found a pair of beaded barrettes

I had wanted. After the lighting of the candles the younger children went to play downstairs in the basement. I sneaked upstairs into Rena and Michael's bedroom. I tiptoed quietly into their bathroom and found the *Penthouse* magazine there. I opened it up and began to read the "Forum" stories. One story was about a woman being forced to have sex with a stranger even though she was married. I read the story and aroused myself on the shag rug until I found the same release that I had at Papa's. The itch I had felt since was scratched. Maybe things would be all right.

My new dance teacher wasn't like other dance teachers. Jenny Fugel was hot. She had hair like Pat Benatar and an attitude like Joan Jett. She was young and hip, and I loved her. She didn't teach us classic ballet; she taught us jazz. Real Fosse jazz. I loved it. Jenny also didn't like to have us dance to classical music; she was fond of rock-and-roll, "Knights in White Satin" by The Moody Blues or "Born to Run" by Bruce Springsteen.

I loved Bruce Springsteen. I already owned "Born to

Run" before I met Jenny, and I'd memorized every word of every song on his new double album *The River*. My favorite song was "Look But Better Not Touch." With his gritty voice and funny lyrics, he really touched me deep inside. I fantasized about being the girls in all his songs. I fantasized about riding away on the back of his bike down "Thunder Road." My friends seemed to like Rick Springfield or Shawn Cassidy more. But I loved Bruce.

One special recital took place after I had been in dance for three years and had advanced so quickly that my teacher was allowing me to do my first solo. It was a jazz number performed to a disco version of "Chattanooga Choo Choo." My costume included denim red-sequined overalls and a train conductor's hat.

My teacher decided to begin the solo with me lying on the stage; I would kick up my feet and arch my back to start dancing. I practiced at home for hours; I was so excited. Mom and Dad were so proud of me; all the family went out for dinner at a restaurant afterwards to celebrate. I remember that for the entire meal my grandfather, Papa, made negative comments about the performance, complaining about how long it was and how bad the dancers were.

During this time, it seemed that Mommy and Daddy were always fighting about money. Daddy said that Mommy thought that money grew on trees. Mommy said she hated being stuck having to have a man to take care of her. She always told me how she was only allowed by Papa to attend junior college and that she wanted me to make sure I was a success on my own, so I wouldn't end up stuck like her.

Daddy got really sick. He lost eighty pounds in a month and was sent to the Joslin Clinic in Boston to be treated for juvenile diabetes. His construction business had failed, and my parents were going broke. They lived in a huge house and couldn't find anyone to pay the price they needed to get for it. Then one part of a solution appeared. My father was offered a great job in Florida.

My parents found a family that was interested in our house. They lived in a neighboring town. Papa had agreed to help my parents out financially so they could move. Everyone in our family knew that Papa was saving them financially. I knew because he told me. Papa reminded me that if I tried to tell about him and what he had done, he would not help my parents.

As all this was happening, I was really worried about Mommy. She was always, it seemed, crying or yelling. She was so upset about the house and the business. Whenever she got the slightest bit upset, I was absolutely terrified. When we were at a restaurant and her food came out wrong, for instance, I felt like I was going to die. I wanted to try to calm her down. It scared me. I felt like something bad was going to happen. I felt like I had to make the situation better. I didn't like her being upset or scared. It scared me. I felt like I had to help her.

CHAPTER 11

I wasn't happy when I heard about the arrangements that had been made for Allison, my brother, and me one night when mahjong was at my mother's friend Marcia's house. My father was away in Florida looking for employment, and the neighbor who usually babysat was not available. My mother asked Hal, Papa's oldest friend, to babysit. He had known the family for years and had known me my whole life. I didn't like him. He was the one I hated to see when he visited us at the Cape, the one who was always pinching me and saying dirty things. He always made me feel scared. Over the years, he had gotten progressively worse. At this point, he was a raging alcoholic, and his wife was leaving him for another man.

That night, his babysitting was practically non-existent. I was the one who changed my brother and ran his bath and put him to bed. Hal just sat on the couch drunk, occasionally grabbing at Allison and me. That night he became extra rough with me. He seemed full of anger. After I put my baby brother to bed, I was singing and dancing with Allison in the main room. We were rehearsing a routine and singing. He grabbed me and said, "You think you are so great." And then he repeated it, sneering, "You think you are so great."

Looking back, I would think that the look of disgust that was probably on my face in his presence would have made any man angry except for the fact that I was only nine years old. Now I realize that his reaction to me, his anger, was as if I were an adult.

He passed out on the couch after grabbing at Allison and me a little bit more. Mom came home from mahjong and went to sleep. As we were still in our big house, where the kids slept in one wing and the master bedroom was in another, it was almost as if my mother were in another house. While I was asleep, the drunken Hal awoke and came into my room.

At first when he woke me, I was scared, and then a sort

of autopilot took over. I looked at this disgusting man in a tee shirt and skivvies and I reached for him, almost in a trance of sleep, to perform the act my grandfather demanded. I was used to that. He grabbed my hair and said, "No way." I started to fully awaken and tried to tell him that I had to go to the bathroom. He didn't let me.

I fought him, but his six-foot frame was too much for me. He was hairy and had a tattoo. He wore a gold necklace that was not unlike Papa's gold necklace. He forced me on top of him and penetrated me. Something was wrong. It was the wrong place. This was bad, very bad. He couldn't do this. I knew because even Papa had told me he wouldn't penetrate me there. I was ruined. All I could think was I might as well die.

I felt myself rise from my body, and I found myself watching the scene from my closet as if I were split from my consciousness. The jabbing was awful. He twisted and pulled at my flat chest. He poked at my sides saying, "Better watch out. Don't want to get any big hips." He touched me, and I found my body jerking uncontrollably. This disgusting creature had caused me to feel pleasure. I was confused. I felt like I was going crazy, going over the edge. My emotions were extremes: fear and anger, hate and sadness. “If you tell anyone,” he said, “I will fucking kill you and your family.”

Hal passed out when he was finished. The bed was wet. I watched him all night long, staring at his big hairy body. I watched each breath move the gray hairs of his moustache. I was paralyzed by the fear that he would awaken and do it again. At some point, I rolled onto the floor quietly and curled up into a ball and cried. When the sun came up, I quietly got my corduroys and sweater and Bass loafers and dressed for school. I looked in the mirror and noticed three things: two bruises on my chest and the fact that my eyes no longer had the light within them that I’d always taken for granted. They looked dull, and I couldn’t make myself look anything but sad. I was ten years old.

At the breakfast table, Hal sat eating breakfast. I could only feel rage and hear the sound of him chewing his food, chewing and chewing. Looking back, I understand that this became a trigger. Whenever anyone anywhere chewed loudly, I burned with rage and wanted to scream.

CHAPTER 12

In sixth grade, students were divided into sections by intelligence. I was in the most advanced section and was separated from a lot of my friends. They stopped talking to me. When I would see them in the cafeteria, they would ignore me. I hated them. Well, not really. But it was easier than accepting that they didn't like me, I suppose. I quickly figured out that to survive in middle school, I was going to have to make some new friends.

The girls in my section were nice but sort of boring. They liked to collect stickers and make ribbon barrettes. It was hard to for me to relate to them because it required me to stuff what I thought of as my wild side way down. My former friends wanted to have boy-girl parties and play spin the bottle. They wanted to listen to AC/DC's *Dirty Deeds* and read *The Joy of Sex*, stolen from their parents. These new girls were different. Their rooms were pretty and sweet.

I became best friends with a neighbor girl who attended private school. Shari was sort of boring, but she would do whatever I wanted, and I liked that. Shari's house was quiet. Shari had an older sister, but that was it. There was never any yelling. Her parents, Brenda and Bob, never fought with each other. They were nice. It was different from my house. Shari was more like a little girl. Her room was full of ribbons and bows. She was definitely less sophisticated than I was. But I liked it there. It was nice. I could forget the truth I now knew, that life is not all pink and sweet, but dark and bad, too.

Some afternoons we would play at my house. The playroom was at the top of a spiral staircase. There was a couch, lots of games, and a real pinball machine. Shari and I would play "dormitory" for hours. We would pretend we were going to college and talk on the phone. Sometimes we would play office and use some of Daddy's old checkbooks. Other times we would play this game where we would tell a story and paste in pieces from old forty-five records. For instance, we would use my new stereo that came with a microphone and tell the story of a woman who fell in love with a prince and then went to a witch who gave them "love potion number nine." We would piece together a whole story that way.

Shari didn't take dance, sing, or play an instrument, but she was really nice. I could trust her. She was safe.

That was the year of the *Preppy Handbook.* I soon picked pink and green to be my favorite colors. I bought shoelaces with little whales or hearts on them. I wore my collar up, and I had Bass loafers and navy chinos.

CHAPTER 13

One night we kids were having dinner at Nana and Papa's. (My father was in Florida during the week.) Papa picked me up at my dance lesson at Town Square. I knew when his gray Chrysler New Yorker pulled up, I was in trouble. Lately he couldn't keep away from me. He wouldn't leave me alone. He tried to control everything I did. He got mad at me for being friends with boys. All I wanted to do was dance and sing, and all he wanted to do was force me to be something else. Perhaps he had no idea that his abuse had caused me to become a freak and no one wanted to be my friend. It was amazing I could talk to anyone at all.

On the ride home that night he didn't say anything, but when we pulled into the driveway, he grabbed my hair and pulled my face down to his lap. It wasn't working. He wasn't getting aroused. I knew what was next. He told me to remove my tights and panties; he put me on top of him, and penetrated me from the rear. It was over quickly. He told me to put my tights back on and go inside and clean up, that Nana would help me. He also said he would keep the panties.

I went inside and went immediately to the bathroom. Everyone else was around the table. Nana came up to me, and I tried to talk to her; I said, "He is going to kill me, Nana."

"No," she said, "Papa loves you; he loves you."

Before leaving the bathroom, I reached down under the sink and took a swig of the White Rain hairspray. I thought that maybe it would help.

I went down to the dining room and sat there, no panties under my tights. It hurt to sit on the chair. I ached; I could not take it any longer. My little brother was in the high chair eating chicken soup, and Allison and Papa were at the table. Nana was cleaning the pots and pans. "I am going to die," I thought. "I really am." I got up and went into the kitchen and again said, "Nana, I am going to die, and he is going to kill me." I reached for the phone. I was going to call my parents and beg them to come home. Nana was holding a frying pan and began to bang me on the head with it, over and over again, shouting as she did: "Stupid. Stupid. Stupid."

Suddenly everything went black. I could not see. I was blind. Nana, realizing what she had done, began to scream. She called my uncle and aunt who came over right away. They took me into the den. I sat on the orange Berber couch with my aunt, and a man with a big black bag came in. Before he finished examining me, my sight returned. "She cannot fall again," he said, "or this is going to be serious. She may become blind permanently."

"Okay," said Nana, and she winked at me.

After all was said and done, my little brother asked for a bowl of chicken soup. It was his first sentence. They were all so excited.

The story of my little brother's first sentence was told many times after that night. It was told over and over until that became the family truth. That became what happened that night.

CHAPTER 14

Hal had gotten drunk again and grabbed his gun and drove his ugly peach-colored Lincoln to pick me up from school. He dragged me by my hair and put me in his car and took me back to his house. When we got there, he pointed his gun at me and made me put on his soon-to-be-ex-wife's lingerie. Then he made me get on top of him, and he raped me again. Afterwards, he offered me some liquor. It tasted good.

I stared out the window at the white sky. Hopeless. I felt utterly hopeless. I heard the voice again from within speak to me. "Close your eyes," it said, "and then look within yourself. This day is like a grain of sand. It is not unimportant, but it is small compared to the rest of your life." Then I was shown a vision of how big my life really was. It was enormous.

By coincidence, Papa was worried about his friend, so he stopped by his house to see how he was. When he walked inside, he saw me. He immediately started calling me a whore. I screamed at him at the top of my lungs: "It's Jennifer, Papa! Jennifer! Your Jenniferl!" He called me a whore again and told me to get dressed.

I put on my tan corduroys and my hand-knit sweater, and he pulled me into the car. Was he kidding? He was taking Hal's side. I was his granddaughter. He loved me. He was supposed to love me. No, he didn't. He couldn't.

He took me back to his house, called my mother, and told her I was sleeping over. He then told Nana that she had to get me ready because he was going to have to purify me. Nana took me upstairs. She put a nightgown on me and told me to wait in bed.

Then Papa came up and said, "I didn't want to have to do this to you. But you are forcing me to." He entered me and the banging feeling in my side lasted only long enough for me to split and land on the popcorn ceiling. I prayed that he would stop. I prayed that Daddy would come home from Florida. I prayed for someone to save me. But no one did.

I made a decision. "If they ever try to touch me again," I thought, "I will kill myself."

CHAPTER 15

Cantor Joe had just announced everyone's part for the Friday night service that the Hebrew-school kids were going to put on. Everyone in class knew that I would get a big part. The whole town knew I could sing. I was assigned the Amidah, the eighteen benedictions in the center of the ceremony. For the next couple of weeks, Hebrew school would take place in the sanctuary, so the children could rehearse.

That same day the foreclosure notice on our house hit the paper. Everyone was gossiping about it. Joey Marcus, who was always mean to me, had a glass eye and would pull it out just to gross me out. He started making fun of me and my father while I was at the pulpit.

"Your father's a loser, and you are going to lose your big house," he chanted. My parents hadn't told me how bad things were. All the other kids just laughed. When I rode the bus home, I stared outside at the white sky and then looked at the kids on the bus with me. "Maybe," I thought, "leaving this place wouldn't be so bad."

Because I was left-handed, my teacher put a plastic thing on my pencil when we began to learn cursive writing. I hated that stupid little attachment, hated that the teacher would call out my name if she noticed that it was missing from my pencil, would walk back to my desk to make sure it was on right. I hated it and hated that I had another thing about me that was different. But that wasn't the only aspect of my life that I hated. I hated everything and everyone. I hated the way my corduroy pants rubbed between my legs, irritating me where I felt raw and damaged. I hated how confused I felt, how lost. I hated how I couldn't keep my stories straight, how I would start to tell my mother something—explain why I didn't want to go somewhere or do something, for example—and I would forget what I had been saying or contradict myself and eventually my words would just trail off.

Actual events and stories I'd heard and daydreams I'd had were fighting for space in my head, and I felt confused and lost. I'd look at the other kids in my class and think that I was supposed to be like them and know that I wasn't but didn't know why. I envied them. I hated them. I worshiped them. I wanted them to like me. Then I'd go back to confusion, sometimes feeling like I was just on the verge of waking up, but could not quite get there.

As we began to master cursive writing, we would try out how we would write our names, practice different looks for our signatures. I'd watch the others form a pretty little signature or try out one that looked dashing or important and, once again, feel different. I was in a quandary; which Jennifer's signature would I adopt? Would it be the geek? The star? The tomboy? Should it be the preppy? How about the whore?

Through the fog of my self-hatred, I focused on just trying to come up with how to write the first letter, the capital "J." I tried out one after another, but couldn't decide. Why was this so hard? What is wrong with me? This shouldn't be such a big deal, I thought, but I couldn't convince myself that it wasn't. Why wasn't I normal? I looked around at the other kids, working away, looking so relaxed. They had no idea what it was like to be me. I could tell by watching them. They looked so young and innocent. They had no idea about how much pressure and stress I was under. I was under it, and it was over me, inside me, all around me. Making that first letter was so hard. I remember realizing that I had to do this, had to at least make the first letter of my name. I bit the inside of my cheek really hard and forced myself to focus on the moment. I tried out several and then chose a simple capital "J" with a big bubble on the top and a small bubble on the bottom. Then I wrote it over and over so I wouldn't forget which one I had chosen.

At home, at night in my bed, I continued a childhood comfort and started sucking my thumb to help me fall asleep. One night I was feeling even more scared and confused and nervous than usual, and I began sucking harder and harder. This turned into little bites when I started using my teeth, too. This led to a very hard bite which was followed by a feeling of relief as this pain I was causing myself somehow made me feel better. I didn't think about it too much or question this; I just felt relieved and glad to be able to fall asleep.

Gradually, this revelation was followed by other practices. I would find myself compulsively biting the skin on the inside of my cheeks. I would pinch my arms hard, so hard I could barely stand it. I dug my fingernails into the tops of my hands and pinched myself as hard as I could.

There were times when all of these failed me. Then I would feel as if I had no choice but to bang my head against whatever surface I could find: a wall, the floor, the back of a door. While I did it, I clenched my jaw and clamped my teeth together so I wouldn't make a sound.

"If you really want to kill yourself, you will cut vertically along your wrist," according to Melissa Goodman. She and her brother Sean were two teenagers who lived on our block. They were known in the neighborhood as bad kids. They drank and smoked cigarettes. Sometimes Melissa babysat for us, and as she and I spent time together, we talked a lot and found a connection regarding the darker realities of life. Melissa told me how she had ended up in the hospital after she took some aspirin when she was going through a really bad time. I listened carefully. The cutting and pinching weren't working anymore. All I felt was hate and rage. And because of our family situation, I didn't want to tell anyone. Couldn't tell anyone. It was apparent that my mother wouldn't be able to handle any more trauma, was barely able to keep on going as it was. She was really a mess.

Not long after Melissa told me about her suicide attempt and gave me the information about the use of a knife, I began to make little trips to my room to visit the knife I kept in my top bureau drawer. I would close my bedroom door, open the drawer, and take out the knife. I would run the tip of the blade along the inside of my arm and then poke the tip at my wrist. I would imagine breaking the skin and feeling relief. I would think that if I sliced myself open, maybe then they would listen to me. Maybe then they would not be angry with me for ruining everything.

CHAPTER 16

The hairs on the back of my neck began to stand up when I heard my mother and father talking not long after Daddy accepted the job he had been offered in Florida. They were discussing the details of resettling, and it became clear to me that my mother was going to go to Florida so that they could find a place for the family to live. I could tell from what they were saying that they planned to leave me and my sister and brother with Nana and Papa. I could feel my body straightening up, my muscles tensing. I was on full alert. I knew I was ready. I felt calm, serious, and strong. No more. I would die first.

Nana and Papa came to stay with us in our house while my parents were gone. Seth Bernstein drove his bike up to my house and sat in the driveway waiting for me to come out. I loved him. He was so cute. Papa was there at the house and saw him pull up. Like some jealous child, Papa gave me a dirty look. Is he crazy? He is my papa. Doesn't Nana see this? Doesn't anyone see this? Papa thinks *he* is my boyfriend.

Nana and Papa invited their friend Hal over, the "friend" who raped me, Hal, whose actions had preceded Papa's cruel reaction of raping me too. They invited him and his girlfriend over to spend the evening.

As soon as I heard about the invitation, I knew I wasn't going to be nice, wasn't going to pretend that everything was all right. I was not, I resolved, going to let him anywhere near me. When they first arrived, I stayed out of the room where they were as long as I could, watching TV. But then he sought me out. As soon as I saw Hal, I started to scream. Nana quickly came into the room. I continued to scream. Allison came in, and I could see she didn't understand what was going on. "Calm down," Nana said, trying to convince me that everything would be okay, that things were different now, that he "was better." She said, "He is our friend. We have to be here for him, be his friends." ("Him? What about me? Who is here for me?" I thought.) I continued to scream.

Nana reached for my hairbrush and started to go for my head. Her hand was raised, the back of the hairbrush poised to slam into me. "No, Nana!" I said, in a loud but controlled voice. I was finally as tall as she was; I looked her in the eye. "I will go blind; don't you remember?" Nana took a step back and turned and left the room.

I went into the bathroom and did what I knew I had to do. Brenda said it would work if I took enough. My hands started to shake as I opened the medicine cabinet and reached for the bottle of aspirin.

I pulled the cap off the bottle and poured aspirin out in my right hand. Then I closed my hand over the aspirin. I got the bottle of rubbing alcohol and used my thumb and index finger to open the bottle of alcohol. I opened my mouth wide and leaned over so I could get the aspirin into my mouth. Then I took a big swig of the rubbing alcohol to wash them down. The next thing I knew, and the last thing I remember from that day, was feeling my face and arms and legs against the hallway carpet and seeing, as if from a few feet above, my body on the carpet.

I woke up the next morning in my bed and found out that help had been summoned to save me. Allison said a fireman came to the house. I was in a very good mood. I felt free and safe and happy and calm. Allison was there, looking terrified. I felt so much love for her; I was overwhelmed by a feeling of how important it was to be her big sister and make her feel better. I asked her to come over to me, and she got up on the bed next to me. "Don't worry, Allison," I said. "I'm okay. When I did it I flew above the clouds and there were people there talking to me. It was beautiful and bright. I am sorry I scared you. It will be okay now."

It was strange, though, as I look back and think about it now. While it was clear that everybody was relieved and happy that I was okay, nobody tried to get me to explain why I had done what I did. (My parents were still in Florida.) Hovering over me as I rested in bed, Nana fluffed my pillows and straightened my sheets. I tried to talk about what I did and how I felt. Something about the look on her face and how she suddenly seemed nervous made me stop and change the subject. I knew my parents needed Papa's help in order to be able to move and make a new start. I knew, of course, because he had told me when he threatened not to help if I told about what he had done.

I was strong enough, I thought. Mommy and Daddy were losing everything, leaving their home. I didn't know the term "nervous breakdown" then, but that day it was clear to me that my mother was in some way sick and that I needed to keep my secrets. I thought that I shouldn't tell her, that I really didn't have to tell her.

Maybe Florida will be different: that was my hope.

CHAPTER 17

For about a week or so, things seemed easier; life was clear. I was pretty happy. But it didn't last. Confusion descended once again. I found myself clinging to little signposts I had figured out that helped me not drown. One thing was that men with mustaches were very dangerous. Here's how I reached this conclusion: Papa had a mustache and Hal had a mustache. What made my theory completely valid was that Daddy definitely didn't have mustache, and Cantor Joe didn't have a mustache. So the mustache quickly became a warning that danger was present.

It got to the point that I was having difficulty keeping everyone and everything straight, and I wasn't sleeping well at all. I was covered in confusion and fear and unease again.

Tolerating others became a matter of gravitating towards those that didn't scare me, and my collection of small details that were important signposts as to safety grew. For instance, even though both Daddy and Hal were tall, Daddy did not have gray hair, but Hal did. Daddy also had a mole on his upper back. I checked for that mole every time he came to tuck me in at night. When I hugged him goodnight, I would place my hand on the part of his shirt where I could feel the little bump of the mole. When I felt the mole, I knew this was Daddy, and I could go to sleep.

Sometimes I listened to music before I went to bed. "Big Balls" was a funny song, but it wasn't my favorite song on the AC/DC *Dirty Deeds* Album. I really loved the title song, "Dirty Deeds," because the sinister man who sang it talked about killing people. Boy, I would think, would I ever like to kill Hal and my grandfather. To just get some justice would be nice.

I remember staring out at the sky and thinking about the possibility of being a singer and dancer. Maybe I would be something else, maybe a lawyer like my Uncle Robert. Then I could get them. I could get them all.

No matter what I did before I tried to go to sleep, I would toss and turn a little and then fall into a sound sleep. Then a few hours later, every night, I woke up in panic. I would sometimes not realize I had been asleep and was waking up until I was already sitting upright, my whole body tensed, my arms clasped together and held tightly against my chest, with both my hands, palms open, one on top of the other, covering my open mouth. I would begin gasping for air and would cup my palms a bit so I could get more air. As my gasping subsided and I was breathing more evenly, I would swing my legs over and put my feet on the floor. Then I'd get up and, even though I felt pretty sure the knife was still there, I would go over to my dresser, and open the upper drawer. I would move the clothes to the front and out of the way and check for the knife I had put there. I would touch it with my fingertips and look at it. Then I'd put the clothes back and start back to my bed. Sometimes I would wake up a few hours later on the floor underneath the bed and then get up and get into my bed. Other times I would get into bed with Allison.

During that time, I never had even one night of uninterrupted sleep.

CHAPTER 18

Finally, it had arrived. Our last day. I stood looking at my bedroom, at all the packing I still had to do. Tomorrow was the day: the movers would be there in the morning. Finally, I was getting out of town, out of my life, away from Papa and Hal and Elaine and everything I had come to hate and fear in this neighborhood, my school, and my life. Maybe now, I remember thinking, maybe in Florida I will be able to sleep through the night, knowing they and all of it were so very far away.

Mom flew down to Florida with my baby brother to meet the moving truck. Allison, Daddy, Grandma, and I would be together on the long ride in the station wagon. I was excited. I could tell the others felt sad, but I just felt relieved and happy. This was a new beginning. I don't remember much about most of the drive. Grandma was nice to be around, was interested in seeing places we drove through and pointing things out to Allison and me. The further away we got from "home," the happier and more relieved I felt.

After we crossed into Florida, I watched as the terrain changed, gradually becoming more and more different from what I had been used to all my life. The trees and plants were different; the sky seemed bigger and brighter. We were so excited when we finally started seeing signs for Fort Myers, but that was nothing compared to how we felt when we drove onto its main street. It was so beautiful. Everything seemed so bright and white and shining and clean. The main street was lined with palm trees that seemed to go up as high as I could see. Daddy drove very slowly, and I tilted my face at the open window, letting the sun warm my face. We were going to have our own swimming pool and live on a golf course. For today, anyway, I was okay. All the badness seemed far, far away.

At one point, a neon sign raised high at the side of the road caught my attention. "God Is Love" it proclaimed.

My excitement about the first day of school in a new town was quickly tempered by the two realities that almost immediately became apparent: Jews were scarce in Fort Myers, and they were not liked. There was one Jewish person on my bus, a boy, and he was very obnoxious and seemed to me to be overly concerned with money and his Polo shirts.

It turned out that Fort Myers, at that time anyway, was a town typical of the Bible Belt, even though it was a bit south of what is typically considered to be that region. Most of the residents were Christian. They did not hesitate to use the word "nigger" to describe black people, something that had been out of favor for some time where I grew up. I was told directly one day by a fellow student who first asked me if I were Jewish that "all Jews are going to hell." Within the first two weeks of school at least one kid asked to see my horns and another, one of the most popular boys in school, threw pennies at me and as they fell to the floor at my feet, yelled, "Pick 'em up, Jew!"

Those demonstrations of anti-Semitism and lack of acceptance were painful, but direct. Others were either less or more subtle and had longer-term impact. The hottest club in school was the Fellowship of Christian Athletes, so, of course, that door was closed to me. Another avenue of acceptance, cheerleading, was closed to me because though I was a performer and trained, I was a dancer and singer and not a cheerleader, not to mention I was a brunette and not the more desirable blond. There was no hope of sitting with the cool kids.

I was, however, placed into the gifted program, and I sat first-chair clarinet in band. I worked hard and did very well in school and quickly made my "smarts" known. If I weren't going to be popular—and although this fact made me angry, that I didn't even have a chance—at least I was going to make a place for myself.

I became friends with a neighbor girl, Debbie Ross. I decided to tell her about a memory I had—a memory that came and went—of being raped. After I told her, she told me never to tell anyone that kind of thing again. She also told me that everyone was sick of me talking about Boston and how everything was in Boston. I stopped talking then.

If anyone asked, I decided to tell only one story and that was that I was so lucky that my Nana and Papa were still alive and were young and loved each other very much. This was the story. I told it over and over again. Sometimes going on and on about how much they cared about each other. I told this story so much it truly became reality for me. The truth succumbed to the story.

The only evidence of the truth was the knife in my dresser, the fact that I couldn't sleep through the night, the fact that I hated the sound of chewing, and the fact that I couldn't stand the sight of any kind of body hair on a man, and the fact that singing and dancing was extremely terrifying, and the fact that I was so angry.

Soon these things just became a part of who I was. That's just you, Jennifer, I told myself. All of it became buried and quiet.

I reminded myself that this was still a place where I did have a chance that I wanted, a chance to leave the past behind. Massachusetts quickly became as far in the past as I could make it. I became a prude, assuming a new identity. I became a member of the geeky sweet clique; I now knew nothing about boys. All the knowledge that had been forced on me I pushed into a corner of the identity I was packaging up and putting away and out of sight and mind. Most of the time, when I was able to handle the anger that was still, I realize now, building up not so far beneath the surface, I was sweet and fun and easy to get along with. Sometimes, though, the anger would appear, unbidden and unwelcome, and I would say or do something mean or cruel. Even though I would usually almost immediately regret my comment or action and quickly apologize and resume my other identity, on some level those present did not forget or misunderstand the depth of the darkness they had seen in that moment. I became known as a snob and a bitch.

CHAPTER 19

Daddy's new job involved building golf communities for adults over fifty-five. He was building a beautiful community with new prefabricated homes and a big clubhouse. He was doing very well. My parents bought a boat, and we soon started going out on the Gulf of Mexico every weekend.

It was so beautiful out there. I loved the sun on my face. It was very important in those days to have a tan and my extremely fair skin would often turn red and peel. It could take weeks to develop a sort of tan, but I persevered in my pursuit.

I loved driving the boat with my dad. Every once in a while when his back was to me, I would momentarily lose track of where I was. When I would return to reality, I would experience a sudden flash of fear. I would quickly locate the mole on his back. When I spotted it, I could relax. It was Daddy. I was safe.

I was afraid to water ski but soon learned to knee board. The water was almost always a beautiful and clear aquamarine; it was easy to see all the way to the bottom. We would all comment on how beautiful and clear it was every time we were out there, as if it hadn't ever been that way before.

Often we would cruise over to Sanibel Island when it was time for lunch. One of us kids would get to drop the anchor when Daddy turned off the motor. Mom would pull out the basket where she had packed sandwiches, chips, and fruit, and we would start passing around drinks from the cooler, soda and juice for the kids and Mom, beer for Daddy. Often the radio blared. Sometimes it would be something currently popular, like the latest Chicago album, and there would be some singing along. Other times it would be quiet while we ate. Often we would be anchored fairly close to the beach, and we'd watch the people who were walking on the beach or playing in the water. It was just the five of us, talking and laughing; sometimes my little brother would say something that would make the rest of us laugh, mispronounce a word or try to tell a joke and not get it right. Mostly he would laugh, too, even though he didn't know what was so funny. If he started to look like he might get his feelings hurt, someone would change the subject, point to sandpipers on the beach or a heron flying overhead or something, and peace would return. I loved it when everything would be quiet and I could hear the little waves lapping against the side of the boat. Sometimes we would see dolphins in the water right next to us, and it seemed as if they wanted to get in on the conversation.

It was paradise.

The author, ages five to seventeen.

CHAPTER 20

In terms of developing my interest in and talent for performing, Fort Myers at that time offered me only two choices: the church choir or beauty pageants. I started dance lessons at a local studio. I became friends with the girls in my dance class. One girl and her sister liked me and the fact that I was Jewish. They invited me to their house. They were born-again Christians and tried to convert me.

My dance coach started training me for beauty pageants. I entered two, Little Miss Sunshine and the Cinderella Pageant.

In preparation for the pageants each girl had to submit a black and white picture of herself. Mom and I went out on the patio, and she took pictures of me. I hated myself.

I hated my smile. I didn't want to smile. My mother kept asking, "What's wrong with you, Jennifer? Why don't you like yourself?" When the pictures came back, I definitely liked the one in which I looked the most angry. In my opinion, I was prettier when I looked angry.

Little Miss Sunshine took place first. The friends I had made came to watch as well as my family, of course, and I belted out "Tomorrow" from *Annie*. I had more experience and training than the other contestants; it seemed that perhaps I had the talent, but not the looks. I took home the trophy for talent, but I lost the overall title to a little blond girl. My friends and family couldn't help but point out to me and to each other that the winner's mother was the pageant's sponsor.

That I had won the trophy for talent was encouraging, though, and I was inspired to put together an even better routine for the Cinderella Pageant. This pageant was big. The winner would continue on to the state competition, and the winner at that level would go on to the national competition. I was excited about the possibilities and determined to succeed.

I worked long hours with my teacher, and we developed a dance routine to accompany a medley of songs from *A Chorus Line.* My mother and I had fun coming up with an idea for my dress for the competition, and my mother found someone to make it for me. It was an off-the-shoulder design made of lavender dotted Swiss, and it was beautiful.

As the day for the event approached, the excitement was at a high pitch. I was so excited, and I felt good because I felt prepared and ready. Everyone from the dance studio was also entering, but no one else was adding the voice component. They were all so nice to me and excited for me, assuring me over and over that I was going to be great, that my performance would win me the title.

On the day of the pageant Mom and I kept to our plan of being completely prepared, and we arrived early, well ahead of the appointed time. We were having fun. We had been amused throughout the preparation by how serious the other girls were about the pageant, how critical winning seemed to them. I knew I was different in other ways, too, as the other girls almost all had curly blond hair and would wear taffeta, but for some reason the contrast didn't bother me at this point. Part of it might have been that I was with my mother, and I was proud of her, especially compared to the other mothers.

Something that did concern me was when I was told that due to the size of the auditorium, I was going to have to use a microphone. I wasn't prepared for this; I had never used one before and the prospect made me nervous. I knew my singing voice was loud, and I was afraid it would be too loud, but I didn't know whether or how to adjust at this point. I was also concerned because I moved a lot as I danced and sang for the routine, and I was afraid it would be hard to hold the microphone as I danced around the stage.

When I stepped out on the stage and the introduction to my music began to play, all my fears fell away and my training and preparation took over. I felt like a star, and I could feel, from the hush of the audience as I began, that the rest of the people in the auditorium felt I was, too. I didn't miss a note or a step. When I finished there was that momentary silence that made me know I had really impressed the audience and then a lot of enthusiastic applause. I felt so happy!

Backstage, my mother hugged me and some of my friends came back to congratulate me. They were all excited and just sure I was going to win. I guess I was, too. But when the winners were announced, my name was called as a runner-up in the talent competition. That was it. My name was not called again.

My mother's disappointment was worse than mine. She drew me aside, away from the friends who were telling me that they couldn't believe I had not won, and began speaking to me in a low voice. "You know," she said, "I'm sure I heard someone backstage whisper that no Jewish girl was going to be Fort Myers' Cinderella."

"It's okay, Mom, really," I said. "Don't worry about it." I suddenly felt more anxious about her reaction than about the pageant.

At this point, we became momentarily separated as some of my friends gathered around me. Then my mother came back to my side, pulling me away from my friends. She was not whispering anymore. "Two people have come up to me and said that you were the best, that it's because you are Jewish that you didn't win."

"Please, Mom, it's okay," I said quietly, trying to calm her down.

"It's not okay!" she exclaimed, her voice getting louder.

"You were the best! Your performance was the best, and you were the best looking girl out there! You know it and I know it and everyone knows it! These damn anti-Semites threw you a crumb with that runner-up trophy. They make me sick! They all make me sick!"

My friends were moving away from us, whispering to each other and giving me odd little looks, mostly sympathetic but a little embarrassed, too. I touched my mother on the arm and told her we should get going. "Stop it!" she shouted. "Don't try to make me be quiet. I hate these small-minded fat idiots and their dumb little blond daughters. You should have won! It's not fair!"

I finally managed to get her out of the auditorium and out to the parking lot. It took her several days to stop talking about my loss and the unfairness of the competition.

I never entered a pageant again.

CHAPTER 21

In the next few years I went up north to Massachusetts a few times. One time was for my friend Shari's bas mitzvah. My family seemed to take it for granted that I would be eager to go back, but it was very difficult to go back, though I did my best to hide my feelings from my parents and my sister and brother. I was far from being excited about seeing all the old places and faces. Actually, I was filled with dread.

It was nice, though, when Shari returned the favor and came down to be at my bas mitzvah. It was a party for 300 and was held at the club house at the country club that my father had designed.

The theme of my party was "Broadway Music." Daddy installed lights that spelled out "Jennifer" and served as the backdrop of the stage. The centerpieces were black and white and red with top hats and sheet music. It was a great party.

As word of the impending party got out, my popularity rating suddenly rose to its greatest height. No one really wanted to be friends with the Jewish kids at school except around the time of their big party. Then all the popular kids buddied up to them so they would be invited.

When Nana and Papa moved down to Florida, to the east coast, I did not want to go visit. Mom didn't make me. I stayed home with Daddy. Mom's first visit to them marked two significant events. I got my first period, and I got caught sneaking out of the house.

When I first saw the spots of blood, I was scared for a minute, but then I realized what it probably was. My mother had not discussed this subject with me, but it had been a topic of discussion with my girlfriends for some time so I kind of knew what to expect. Actually, at this point, another girl and I were the only ones who hadn't yet reached this milestone. I knew there were special pads to wear to deal with this, but I didn't have any; Daddy took me to get some.

Our neighborhood was a combination of homes that backed up to either golf courses or creeks. One time some friends and I decided to sneak out onto the golf course and play, and pretty soon we were doing this every weekend. It was so exciting. The boys in the neighborhood would hide six packs of beer tied to ropes at the bottom of one or other of the creeks. We girls would go with them and drink the warm, cheap beer. I loved the beer from the first sip. No more stress. No more anger. I wasn't afraid. The moment that the alcohol hit me I was free. Sometimes nobody could get beer, and we had to raid one of the parents' liquor cabinets. We would only take about a third of the liquid from each bottle and replace it with water so the parents wouldn't find out.

Shawn Carp, my partner for these adventures, was really cute. He was also dating the most popular girl in school and normally wouldn't even have looked at me. But on the golf course he did. He did a lot more than look. Over Christmas break, we all sneaked out almost every night. It was during that period that after some warm beer, Shawn Carp gave me my first French kiss. He gave me quite a few kisses over that break. I loved it and relived those nights throughout the next day, anticipating the next night. I would roll my tongue around my mouth, trying to duplicate the sensation of our kissing.

When we returned to school after Christmas break, I was still under the spell of all those nights on the golf course. Shawn told his girlfriend, who was a cheerleader and thus one of the popular crowd. She immediately declared war on me. She used her influence on the cheerleading squad and convinced some of the girls to go after me. They followed me home on the bus and pushed me around at school. It was terrifying. But, at the same time, I felt it was well worth it. No way was I going to let anyone tell me to turn down beer and French kisses from Shawn Carp. No way!

Things settled down for me at school, and I made friends with a girl who also had made the most popular girls' enemies list. We bonded instantly as a result of our mutual needs and complementary situations. First, of course, we were both considered outsiders by the popular group at school, but Laura was gorgeous, a cheerleader, and a Christian. Her family struggled financially and was headed by a divorced working mother. She had two brothers. I had an intact family with two parents and had money to share. It was a match made in heaven. I taught Laura about Bruce Springsteen; she taught me about White Snake and Journey.

The first summer we were friends, I was scheduled to go to a Jewish camp in the Poconos. Before I left, Laura and I spent lots of time together spraying our hair with Sun In and getting burnt to a crisp. Occasionally we would go to the roller skating rink, the mall, or the movies.

This trip up north was much better than the last. Camp was awesome. I left the torrid world of born-again-

Christian land and entered the world of the Long Island Jewish American princess. These girls were awesome. They loved me and accepted me immediately because I was cute and could sing and dance. I felt I was one of them, not an outsider like I was in Florida. I loved them because they taught me about Madonna, Run DMC, Guess jeans, and Forenza sweaters. They had some serious style. They knew all about Gucci and Louis Vuitton. They wore Swatch watches and big Rayban glasses. I borrowed their clothes and put their tapes in my Walkman.

I had a sweet boyfriend from Miami. We would go to the dances and the canteen together and dance and make out by the lake. One more thing. It seemed that all Jewish boys from New York and New Jersey loved Bruce Springsteen.

This was heaven! I had found a whole camp full of soul mates.

When I returned to Fort Myers after my wonderful time in camp I was starting my freshman year in high school. I had found a little more self-confidence. The girls at camp had taught me some fashion, music, and style. It didn't seem to matter as much that I didn't fit in. Camp friends kept in touch all year. All year I could look forward to going to camp again.

I brought Laura back some of the black rubber Madonna bracelets I got while I was away. I was so happy now and looking forward to high school. I remember thinking "this year is going to be great!" Laura would be a cheerleader here, too, so it would be fun to go to the football games and watch Laura. It would be fun just to be that much a part of what was going on.

Laura knew how to do everything. She knew how to use a tampon. She knew how to put on eye shadow. She knew how to shave pubic hair for wearing a bikini. And boys liked her. Boys weren't too interested in me; I was still just the awkward little Jewish girl. But I loved them. Especially one of the senior football players that I thought was just unbelievably wonderful. He was dating one of the senior cheerleaders. He made my heart jump. I would walk all the way around school in between classes just to walk by him casually and smile, as if I just happened to be in the same hallway.

Daddy didn't have any pornography in the house so I had to get creative to masturbate. I found a paperback book that had a piano teacher seducing a student, a much younger person. This scene provided all the elements I needed.

Even though we had moved and my linens were new, my bedroom furniture was the same. The same four-poster bed where Hal had raped me and the same dresser that was part of the setting of that horrible night. I still couldn't sleep through the night. I would wake up every single night and either sneak into Allison's room or my little brother's room or go to the couch in the den. I still had a knife in my top drawer.

My parents took our family on a three-day cruise out of Miami and I met Donny Stevens, a Jewish boy from San Jose. He was cool. He listened to Black Flag and The Sex Pistols. While we were watching the movie *Purple Rain,* he touched my breasts and then put his hand down my pants. He was older and more experienced. He got me tipsy and went down on me. He knew what to do and how to do it. I had an orgasm while Morris Day was doing the Bird. In that instant, I fell in love with Donny Stevens.

During ninth grade we flew up to Massachusetts for a family event. We took time to visit both sides of the family. We spent one afternoon with my Dad's family eating fresh fried clams. Then we met my mother's family at Uncle Jeff's house for Chinese food. Everyone was asking me what I was going to do about college. I explained that I wanted to go to New York to do musical theater. First Papa exclaimed how stupid that was, that no one ever made a living as an artist. I asked everyone there if they thought I was good enough, if they thought I could do it. Not one person there thought I could. I was so angry. I pushed the anger way down deep. I hated them all. But then I thought what's the use? Maybe they were right. Maybe I wasn't good enough. I really didn't want to visit them anymore.

I had never learned how to express anger. Because any sign of anger was shamed with a "not nice" or "a bitch" comment, I was unable to communicate with anyone when I was angry. This made it difficult for me to keep a friend for a long period of time. I was controlling of all those around me, and I wanted them to do what I wanted. Then I felt safe. If someone did not do what I wanted him or her to do, I got mad. However I was unable to tell this to the other person, so I became the master of the evil eye. I wanted the person to know I was angry. I wanted the other person to figure it out. But when that person didn't figure it out, couldn't read my mind, I would conclude that he or she did not care. The relationship would end in a wall of resentment, a wall I had created.

CHAPTER 22

Unfortunately, the old saying "the only way out is through" is true. You can't just bury your memories of abuse. At this point, I had no consistent conscious memory of the sexual violence and the emotional and physical pain and the heartbreak of what I had suffered at the hands of Papa, Hal, Elaine, and, yes, Nana. The memories were obscured by a constant stream of anger and resentment. This anger and resentment caused an extreme amount of psychic pain. I found only five things that relieved that pain: unhealthy love connections, gossip and judgment of others, material things, sexual release, and marijuana or alcohol.

At the same time in the same way that alcohol may seem to help a person to go to sleep only to cause wakefulness after a few hours of sleep, my coping mechanisms helped me lose my pain at first only to open the door wide to that pain later. While I can see that so clearly now, that truth was not accessible to me in my years of frenzied attempts to escape from the past. What I focused on then was the immediate release from pain, not the rebound effect and resurfacing-of-pain stage.

When I drank, as I first experienced during those evenings on the golf course with the beer hidden in the creeks and attention from another girl's boyfriend, I became in my mind seemingly magically the more-acceptable blond—and beautiful. Most of all, I was at ease, unafraid to be the center of attention, not afraid to be something closer to what at that time passed for myself. Drinking, I was not afraid of my power or my sexuality: my body was not the "enemy." Even when the daytime brought retribution—from that boy's girlfriend or through gossip about me or however—I didn't put down alcohol. Alcohol was my friend.

Not only that, alcohol truly was magic for me, I thought. One time I took my friends out in a limo, flashing lots of money, getting drunk and very physical with a popular boy who normally would never give me the time of day.

Yes, alcohol was magic and it was my friend. It would be quite a while, and I would experience a lot of pain and destruction, before I could see beyond those attractions.

When my history and unresolved pain from the past abuse collided with the changes and anxiety that are part and parcel of adolescence, one of my reactions was to become whomever I thought people wanted me to be. I was not a real person but a shell of one, a chameleon. I would watch movies and quickly change my hair and clothing to match the hair and style of the star. I had many personalities; I had learned from incest to become different people, and now I took this skill to a new level. I became addicted to clothing and jewelry, how I looked on the outside. In high school I actually got an award for never wearing the same outfit twice.

As part of this phase, I became argumentative regarding religion. I became angry at all faiths. While many adolescents raised in a certain faith may question or reject at least for a while the religion they have grown up in, I became angry with all of them. My parents attempted to keep us connected with Judaism with bas and bat mitzvahs and other rites and observances, summer camp, and their devotion to Israel.

One part of my response to their efforts was that Judaism took a new and different role in my life. I wore it as a badge of victimhood. I was a victim, born and bred. A paranoid victim of anti-Semitism. Even as I reveled in being able to be a victim outwardly—though I kept the real source of my status to myself—I had a certain sense of superiority. I knew so much more than my friends or my family or my rabbi or my teachers. I knew the truth. Deep within me I had knowledge none of them could comprehend. I knew the dark truth about life.

I was smart and pretended to be a big prude. I judged and criticized everyone. The shame of being a victim of incest was instantly doubled by being a Jew. And it was here in Ft. Myers I was first exposed to the concept of burning in hell. I was going to hell. Definitely. No way anyone with my secrets could escape that fiery fate.

In addition to my own personal, partly normal adolescent, partly incest-influenced rebellion regarding religion, the possibility of faith-based help for my pain was complicated by another factor: the Jews in Ft. Myers made it very clear that it was important in this town not to act "too Jewish." This sense seems to have permeated the very roots of the religion in the area, even in the privacy of the temple. I was surprised to realize that I knew more of the liturgy than the rabbi. It was a shock.

Then, too, I understand now, floating in the deep background of all this must have been the fact that the predator in the central fact and drama of my childhood, my maternal grandfather, Papa, the man who brought so much evil and pain into my life, was a pillar of our temple then, probably almost seemed to me to be a shadow of one of the Patriarchs. It would only be much later that I would be able to allow this fact to enter my consciousness and to come to terms with it, to not only surrender myself to my faith, but to find deep consolation there.

I cared about singing and dancing until I found alcohol. Then alcohol took over, and I eventually began using marijuana as well. It was way more important for me to feel comfortable and accepted than to be creative. It wasn't cool to be in the marching band, so I quit playing clarinet. I just concentrated on social life; my focus was all on being accepted, stuffing everything painful down, deeper and deeper until it disappeared.

I was still masturbating daily for release. I was a prudish, geeky, know-it-all snob during the day and a wild-woman pervert at night. I lived a double life, and I felt the stress of living this fragmented existence every moment that I was not lost in my addictions.

Mommy hated Ft. Myers. The anti-Semitism and everything else. A teacher of mine recommended the town of Sarasota. It had a renowned high school for the performing arts and a special public school for the gifted. I was furious. I had spent the last three years figuring out a way to be acceptable to this place, and now we were going to have to move again. We were to move after summer camp. Daddy bought us a house on Siesta Key, a little north of Ft. Myers and a stone's throw from a gorgeous beach. We even had a canal in the back of our house for our two boats. I came around to accepting the move and started thinking "how bad could it be?" Plus summer camp had been so much fun.

Not long after school started, I began dating an older boy who would become my sweetheart. On our first date together I got drunk and told him I had been molested. He asked me about it, and I pretended it was nothing.

I went to visit my closest friend in Ft. Myers for the weekend and got really drunk and had my first blackout. I woke up with a hickey on my neck and was petrified of what my sweetheart would say. He forgave me, but I never went to visit that friend again.

My drinking was clearly different than my friends' drinking. By tenth grade I was a daily pot smoker and weekend binger. My friends would try to limit my drinking to a four-pack of wine coolers to ensure I wouldn't do anything crazy. I continued to binge and black out throughout the rest of high school. I also continued to act out sexually through masturbation and being stroked by others.

(I didn't lose my virginity until twelfth grade: my

sweetheart and I lost our virginity to each other. It was a planned and special evening. Even as I write that statement, I realize once again just how "double" my life was. I truly felt that Jennifer the high-school senior was losing her virginity. What little-girl Jennifer, the victim of incest and other sexual assault, had lost was something in another realm completely.)

I had many boyfriends at summer camp and in school. And I needed them all and the attention they gave me to fill the never-ending emptiness that was growing within me.

On school days, I started at the public high school at 8:00 a.m., and then in the middle of the day took a bus to the performing high school to study music. It was awful. I dreaded the idea of making new friends. I couldn't bear the thought of having to navigate my way through another big high school. I told my mom, and she had me placed in the school for the gifted where my sister and brother were both enrolled. Pine View School for the Gifted was an unusual but cool place. My entire class consisted of sixty-nine people. Not a lot of navigating to do.

The entire school was housed in portables, the temporary buildings other schools used for overflow classes. Things at Pine View were great, so great that I hated to have to get on the bus to the performing-arts high school in the middle of the day. Going there also meant that I didn't get home until close to five o'clock at night. Plus, everything they were doing was boring to me. I had already studied music theory at music camp. And, frankly, I was enjoying my new school. At Pine View everyone was a little unique; it was, after all, a school for the gifted. The bar for popularity was not so high. People pretty much accepted you as you were. Also, there were Jewish kids, and I had a boyfriend soon after I arrived. I had great friends who accepted all my quirks. About halfway through tenth grade one of the coolest senior boys sent his friend to talk to one of my friends at a local football game. He wanted to know my name.

He was so cute. He looked like Bono from U2 and dressed every day in black Rayban sunglasses and a trench coat. He was interested in me. That weekend my friends and I went to the beach, and he was there. He pulled his glasses down and looked at me. I thought I was going to die. He was a member of Key Club at school, so my friend and I joined. He asked me one day during lunch if he could give me a ride that night to the Key Club meeting. I had a boyfriend, but this guy had a car. So my boyfriend got pushed aside and John picked me up. He drove a white Cutlass Supreme. The ceiling fabric was peeling down, so he held it up with pins representing various rock groups: INXS, Smiths, U2, The Police. This was awesome.

After the Key Club meeting he took me home and asked me out on a date. I said yes. Our first date was to some stupid Chevy Chase movie, but who cares. I got to walk around the mall with him. It was awesome. John kissed me that night and every other night almost for the next three years. John wasn't Jewish, didn't come from a family like mine. But it was puppy love. He completely loved and accepted everything about me. He didn't care that I absolutely hated anyone who chewed loudly in my ear. He didn't care that I sucked my thumb to go to bed. He also didn't care that I wanted to wait to go all the way. He loved me. And for the first time I felt loved and okay.

John also didn't care that occasionally I got drunk

and high and would maybe cheat on him. He would pick me up many a Saturday night after a night of drinking with my friends. He was always there. I was filled with so much anger for everyone. The only thing that relieved it was masturbation, pot, or booze. My friends would just joke about how angry I was all the time. They also would comment on how the pot made me more fun and relaxed. They were right.

Even in Sarasota, I didn't sleep through the night. John would often hold me until I fell asleep.

The summer before senior year my parents decided that this summer I would go to Israel for the summer. I didn't want to go. I didn't want to leave John. We all drove as a family up the East Coast and dropped my sister and brother off at camp, and then my parents took me to JFK airport to EL AL to go on a tour for the summer. I was crying when I left. I did not want to go. Daddy said I would thank him for it, that it would be great.

Israel was torture at the beginning. For the first two

weeks all I wanted was to go home to see John. But in Israel there is no minimum age for drinking alcohol, plus over the summer there are thousands of teenagers from all around the world visiting, so it became rather fun. We hiked through the desert, climbed Masada, and walked through the water tunnels. It was beautiful. I hit a serious low with my drinking.

We were down in the southern tip of Israel at the resort town of Elat when I had too much to drink and blacked out for the fourth time on the trip. My tour guide was worried and sat down with me to talk to me about it. My friends were concerned because I had vomited in my sleep that night; they got me up and helped me shower. They said I was saying all these vile things. I could not remember any of it. I wasn't concerned. I fooled around with lots of boys and continued to drink excessively until I got back to the United States.

Senior year was great, and I was accepted to my dream school: University of Massachusetts. The only drawback was that John was not going to be there. He promised to apply to one of the schools nearby. At the graduation ceremony I sang the song "The Rose" and cried. (And I remember thinking—in my state of detachment from reality—"Why am I crying?")

My plan was to study to be a biochemist. I was going to invent an artificial pancreas to cure Daddy's diabetes. I was still smoking pot every day. I was still drinking as much as I could. I was still acting out sexually and I was still bullshitting everyone I could with the million masks I wore. I was filled with rage and hate. I did not have any idea who I was. I was lost.

CHAPTER 23

I graduated from high school, a gifted stoner alcoholic who never wore the same outfit twice.

I left to attend the University of Massachusetts. In college my drinking grew into a monster that controlled my life. I almost failed my first semester due to drinking and pot use. I quickly changed my major and joined a sorority in an effort to solve my problems. Unfortunately, I took "me" into the sorority. It was an especially difficult environment for wild-woman Jennifer's personalities. It is hard to masturbate daily living in a small room with three other girls. It's hard to sleep around when the Greek community is so small. I quickly earned the enmity of my sorority sisters.

I was truly one girl during the day and another one at night. My sorority sisters called me Sybil. My alcoholism caused me to black out weekly, vomit, and wet my bed. When I drank, I quickly turned violent. I would physically beat up whatever male was in my immediate vicinity. I used swear words. I would hear about my behavior the next day because at some point in the festivities, I would have blacked out. My boyfriend made me agree to drink only Shirley Temples at his fraternity's formal before he would agree to let me attend it with him.

It was classic Jekyll and Hyde. There were two of me, and I knew it. Deep inside I knew I was crazy. There was the weak one and then there was the strong person who would tell me to get up. She would scream at me to get me through everything. When I drank, these two parts began to fight. I can remember a few times before blacking out and before having sex with some guy when I would be totally drunk screaming at myself: "Get up. Go in there and get him." And I would and then I would sneak home and pass out and wake up with shame and blank spaces in my memory of the evening.

The good Jennifer held sway often enough that I did

manage to be a member of the All State Chorus at the university, and I performed in one musical production for the theater club. Even so, I began having panic attacks. I tried to hide them. I thought I was going crazy.

The DJ at the local dance club was a cocaine dealer. One night as a long shift wore on, I was sleepy. My friend, a bartender there, suggested I try some cocaine. I did. In my fingernail like I had seen in the movies. It was awful. I felt like I was going to have a heart attack. I never touched it again. Thank God.

When I transferred from the University of Massachusetts, it was really due to, I realize now, a kind of emotional breakdown, but I was able to keep this secret from my family. I was still good at keeping secrets and playing roles I had created for myself. I suppose they were used to my position in the family and were able to or perhaps had to believe I was as I appeared to be. I was so good at keeping everything secret from them. Incest and addiction kept me separate from them now as it had for nearly my whole life. I lied to my father; I told him I didn't like the snow anymore and that I didn't want to be in college anymore. He knew someone at a local college in Florida and got me a quick interview. I began taking classes there almost immediately. I entered as a junior.

I was now officially a theater major and remained one for the next two semesters. I also joined the chorus at this school and performed with them at Lincoln Center in New York City. That's the outward story. Inwardly, I was still lost. My alcoholism and sex addiction—they had been quiet, in hiding, as I adjusted to my new life—reasserted their power over my actions. I would think I was going to spend the weekend studying and even refuse an invitation or two. Then I would find myself having a drink with someone, like one of my friends' sort-of boyfriend in one instance, telling myself that I would just have one or two drinks and go home. I would end up letting things go further and further until I'd wake up drunk and disoriented and, in the case of my liaison with my friend's sort-of boyfriend, pregnant. I had my first abortion. After that, my friend's sort-of boyfriend and I got engaged.

Some part of me knew this relationship was not good for me, was not taking me in the direction I needed to go, but I drowned those feelings: we drank and/or smoked pot almost every day. I began having panic attacks again, and they quickly became more powerful than before. My boyfriend had to rush me to the hospital many a night only to have to wait with me for a long time and then make the return trip with me when the doctors sent me home. During sex with this boyfriend I started having flashbacks of my incest; I tried very hard not to share this fact with him. When we would have sex, I would see hair on his chest, hair that he did not have.

I made a feeble attempt at psychotherapy. I went to a psychotherapist and was given a long test. The diagnosis? Paranoid schizophrenia.

I changed my major one last time and in a moment of grace, that inner voice, the one that has at times directed my better actions, drew me to two classes: African American Women Writers and American Women of Poetry. In these classes I discovered Zora Neal Hurston, Alice Walker, Emily Dickinson, and Anne Sexton. These women inspired me to find my own voice.

In the last year of college with these two classes, I began to write, and through the process of writing, I began to change. Unfortunately, I approached my writing the same as everything in my life and almost immediately was writing compulsively, in binges. I would stay up all night and write poetry. One memorable episode involved me locking myself in my room and writing, in just two hours, a screenplay about incest.

My boyfriend and I were both worried and amazed. I had found something I could do. Writing seemed to be easy. However, as I see it now, I did not have the necessary sense of self-worth at that time to take myself seriously enough to work at becoming a poet.

I went back to visit some friends at my school up north and got drunk, got pregnant, and came home. I had my second abortion.

CHAPTER 24

I was sure that I loved writing, but I did not see how I could support myself by writing. Most people who are interested in writing as undergraduates have heard that law is a good choice for students who can write; in addition to that background whisper was perhaps some memory of my sense at one point in my childhood that if I went into law, I could defend myself, even punish my abusers. Whatever else there might have been influencing me at this point, I made a decision: I would apply to law school.

I studied hard for the boards and was accepted into law school on scholarship. The summer before I left for law school I traveled to Fire Island, New York, for a vacation. I drank so much on this trip that I seemed to have become psychotic. I found myself alone with a knife, trying to kill some imaginary man. I was so tormented. Once again, I had started out thinking that I would have a nice break and enjoy myself before settling down to working diligently and moving forward in my life. Once again, my first drink, accepted as if I could have some casual drinks, relax, and still control myself, was a trap door through which I tumbled and fell back into the land of the lost. As I recovered from the episode I was, once again, almost consumed with regret, shame, and guilt.

That vacation was a portent of things to come. As I entered law school, I was still with my boyfriend from college, but that relationship was not to last long. Despite my ambition and intentions, my alcoholism became part and parcel of my law school experience. My grades were poor; I lost my scholarship.

What I now understand to have been my sexual addiction played out as I, without fully intending to, cheated on my boyfriend. I contracted herpes. A whole new level of shame began to eat away at me. I was finding it harder to look in the mirror. The only cessation of pain and shame and self-loathing I could find was in pursuing my two addictions.

Then when I would emerge from another bout of losing myself, the pain and shame returned with renewed strength. I had to fix this. I had to figure it out. "Law school. That's it!" I thought. "That's what is causing my misery. The pressure is too much." I dropped out.

My boyfriend continued with law school while I worked at a coffee shop. I continued drinking and acting out sexually every day. My addictive activities were the true focus of each day, though I was still under the impression that I was in control and would be changing things soon.

At this point I left my boyfriend, moved back to my undergraduate town, and got my own apartment. I got a job as a waitress for a large restaurant chain. I discovered the easy high of inexpensive wine and that I could go out to bars by myself. After the strangeness of the first time, going to a bar alone became a little private pleasure, walking in and finding a spot to sit, ordering a drink and watching people, then watching them watch me. Then, of course, I would turn to the real reason I was there: to drink myself into oblivion.

My days assumed a certain rhythm and routine: I'd work the lunch shift and then use my tips to cover the previous night's bar tab and buy a box of wine. I had to have at least a box a day as wine became another member of my collection of obsessions.

I made my way quickly through a few waiters on the restaurant's staff, finally ending up in a cozy relationship with one of the alcoholic cooks. Conveniently, he lived within walking distance of our favorite bar; almost immediately we were there together every night. It might have seemed that my life was settling down into a stable and productive routine, but that appearance was deceptive. Actually, my escalating drinking began to result in many embarrassing situations. Once again, I began trying to find reasons for the negative effects, to analyze and fix the situation. "Ah, it's the beer I'm drinking. Quit that beer. I'll drink ice beer. Hmm, well, maybe it's the ice beer. I'll try no beer, hard liquor only. Hmm, that's not it, either." I tried everything, every way to manage alcohol to avoid blacking out. I was practically a black-out-cause scientist, lost in my work. Nothing helped. The situation escalated. One drink and I was drunk.

Daily, I was also acting out sexually at that time. I discovered the vibrator. What a convenience! I no longer had to worry about finding porn or taking the time to fantasize to get aroused. A few seconds with the vibrator brought release. Soon, however, an unfortunate side effect surfaced. The stress of using it over and over again made my herpes breakouts almost constant. Nevertheless, I refused to give up my masturbation. Actually, it was not so much a matter of refusal: the truth of it is, I was powerless, unable to stop.

My stressful and dangerous routine continued until one night when I was drunk and standing outside my favorite bar. As I remember, I had not been thinking at that moment about my life or, really, about anything. I was just standing there, feelings numb, staring out at the passing traffic. All of a sudden, I heard the voice, the voice that was not mine, the one that had directed me in the past. "Go back to school," it said. Just like that, out of the blue, "Go back to school." It was almost like I suddenly recovered myself for a moment. "What am I doing?" I said aloud, to myself. "What am I doing?"

I turned and walked back to my boyfriend's apartment, kicked off my shoes and got into bed, not bothering to remove my clothes. The next morning, before I did anything, I found the number for the law school I had left and called the dean's office. I got through to her right away and asked her what I had to do to return to school. She got my record up on her computer and told me I could come back, but that in order to do so I would have to prove myself by making the Dean's List my first term back. If I did so, that would bring my grade-point average up to where it needed to be so that I could stay in school. "I can do it," I said and started making arrangements as soon as I got off the phone.

My cook boyfriend and I went back to my law school together. We quickly secured positions close to the school at a branch of the restaurant chain where we had met. I was determined to take school seriously this time; I drank and smoked marijuana only on weekends. I waitressed and I studied. I got close to a couple other members of the restaurant staff who told me they were sober and in recovery in a twelve-step program, something I had never heard of until they told me about it.

By my second semester back, I had made the Dean's List twice, and my future as a law student seemed secure. This I took as license to party. I began drinking wine heavily again, every day. My condition had progressed substantially. I was now drinking whiskey and coke in a nearby bar with a select group of law school alcoholics. I was constantly having panic attacks. One afternoon, I was driving home from an afternoon class and was forced by my feelings to stop and drink. Was alcohol or anxiety to blame? Probably, it seems now, both. I didn't understand why; all I knew was that I had to stop and drink. Right then.

Soon, I was cheating on my boyfriend, who was now my fiancé. I was waking up and throwing up. I was going to class drunk and having fender benders in the parking lot. I was a mess. I secured a great law-clerk position that paid well, but I was so hung over when I was working that I was unable to give the job what it required. More and more often my hands would shake, and I was unable to make them stop. I was exhausted. Alcohol was once again taking over my life.

CHAPTER 25

The very last time I had a drink, I was at a party. I was still in law school, but my addictions were now a major part of my life again. When I walked into the party, I was already so drunk and stoned that I could not feel my legs. I headed immediately for the keg. I picked up a cup and was about to reach for the tap. Suddenly, my world shifted. I was still at the party; I was still standing in front of the keg. That is, my physical being had not moved. However, an essential part of me—my intelligence, heart, spirit, everything but the physical—was free and was high above the room, viewing it all from the chandelier. I suddenly had a grand panoramic view of myself. For the first time, I saw it all. The lying, the drinking, and the sexuality as connections to oblivion, the lack of concern for others and myself, how I kept trying to tell myself to stop and continued to fail. I was terrified and disgusted.

As I returned to my physical self, I finished reaching for the tap and quickly got a drink, then another and another. I got angry with one of my friends for what seemed to be no reason at all, then got my keys and tripped and fell against parked cars as I found my way to my car. My out-of-body experience kept replaying itself as I drove home. I was convinced that it meant I was about to die. Part of me was afraid, but mostly I did not care. I couldn't think my way out of this.

I was so drunk that I could not feel the steering wheel or the pedals of the car. There were no lights on Flamingo Road then, and I swerved often. I stared at the dividing line in the middle of the road whenever it was illuminated by sudden lights from another car or when the moon came out from behind the clouds. I began to pray. "Please, God, get me home," I said out loud, over and over.

The next morning I woke up slowly, neatly tucked in my bed as if nothing had happened. When I sat up, the severe hangover I would suffer from that day signaled its presence through the pounding pain in my head and the uneasiness in my stomach. I looked over at my fiancé. "Never again," I said, "I am never drinking again."

"You always say that," he said.

But this time was different. I moved my legs carefully over the side of the bed, put my feet on the floor, and stood up cautiously. I walked slowly to the phone and was glad to see that the phone book was in plain sight so I wouldn't have to look for it. I looked up a twelve-step organization and listened to a recording that after a short message, gave me the option to hear a list of meeting times and locations. I was too weak to figure out which one to go to, but I felt secure knowing that I could find one when I was able to go.

Hours later, I took a shower and found some clean clothes and went to the restaurant to see my friend who was in recovery. I asked him if he could go with me the next day to a meeting. "Of course," he said, and he hugged me. I went home and slept and woke up the next morning, focused only on getting to the meeting.

CHAPTER 26

At my first meeting I cried. Almost immediately I became a solid member of recovery. I joined a home group and went to meetings every day. At the first meeting a kind older man invited me to go the next night to a meeting called the Happy Hour. I went to that group on that Monday at five-thirty and every Monday through Friday at five-thirty for the next three years.

This meeting became my home group. At this home group I was not allowed to share, as I knew nothing about my disease of alcoholism, but I was allowed to listen and talk for hours to anyone after the meeting. All the men and women shared their feelings and experiences. I identified with them immediately. I was adopted by a sweet nurse named Gloria who became my temporary sponsor. Gloria told me to call her every day. When I got home every night, I called her just to check in.

At my home group they raffled off books regarding addiction and recovery and the program every day. I seemed to win just about every time I needed a new one. I started reading the basic text of the program and working my program. Soon I became the raffle-ticket seller, and after a while I was trusted to make the coffee. During this time I was still studying hard and finishing up law school.

The focus of my day-to-day life became law school and meetings. I got a sponsor who took me through the steps. I began to clean up my past. I made amends to my family and to my friends. Slowly, carefully, day by day and step by step, I began to move away from the hell I had been living in and learned to value integrity, honesty, and responsibility.

A woman in my home group shared with us that that every time she saw a rainbow, she knew that her higher power was present. I started looking for rainbows. I soon began to spot them all the time.

CHAPTER 27

Sober, I was able to graduate from law school and pass the bar. I also fell in love with a wonderful friend who understood my recovery. This man would become my husband.

I first became friends with Spencer my first semester back, the semester I stopped drinking and smoking pot and just worked and studied. He was preppy and smart. He was Jewish and dated a lot of girls. He was confident and very good looking. The law was natural to him. It just happened that we had almost every class together, and we became friends. I was on academic probation, and Spencer was ranked number two in the class. He taught me about how to take a law school exam.

Spencer ran with a different crowd than I did. The rich crowd. They drove nice cars and partied on South Beach. My friends smoked pot and watched Melrose Place every Monday night together. But in spite of these differences, we became really good friends. I got good grades and made Dean's List and was able to stay in law school. Still, I thought that Spencer wasn't my type. Maybe I thought he was too good.

About ninety days into my sobriety I was in a trial practice class with Spencer, and suddenly I saw him differently. I felt interested in him. ("When did that happen?" I thought.) He invited me out with his friends; I was a little nervous because I knew there would be drinking. He knew I was sober and seemed to understand.

I dressed up that night for the first time in a long time. I thought I looked pretty good. I wore a short black dress with a mock turtleneck, black tights, and black heels. We were sitting in his car, and I decided I would tell him that I had feelings for him. He cut me off and said he didn't have to be reminded any more that "we were just friends." I laughed because he had no idea how I was feeling. The next morning he and a friend were entering a big trial competition. I decided to tell him my feelings in a note and leave it for him to find. He did great in the competition and, afterwards, found the note. We started dating.

Our dating consisted mostly of playing cards, smoking cigarettes, studying for law school, and twelve-step meetings. I went every day, and if Spencer wanted to be around me, I just decided he would have to deal with it. I was still working at the restaurant.

I had difficulty finding employment after graduation, so I was forced to stay at the restaurant. I also worked as a volunteer for the area legal aid office. This turned out to be just what I needed. Working with other lawyers kept me focused on the discipline of law, and because it was not a full-time professional position, I had time to continue with the work of recovery, as Gloria reminded me at the time. In my first year of recovery I began to journal and write again.

After I had six months of sobriety, my mom called to tell me that Papa had throat cancer. I drove home to Sarasota three hours each way almost every weekend to see him. On every drive home I had at least four panic attacks. Why? I did not know. (The violence of my childhood was hidden from me at this point.) Maybe I was just crazy, I told myself. Papa had a three percent chance to live. He started serious chemotherapy, and Spencer and I were there with my parents and Nana through all of it. He went into remission soon after. It was a miracle.

We graduated from law school and began studying furiously for the bar exam. On the second day of the bar exam I lost my car keys in the middle of the test, during a break. The entire second part of the test I was terrified because I had my friend Sally's luggage in my trunk and she had to leave right after the exam to go to New Jersey to take the bar exam there. I later found out that Spencer was worried, too, for another reason.

We had agreed to drive to Disney World so I could bravely ride my first roller coaster: Space Mountain. The security guard found my keys, and off Spencer and I went to Disney World. On the way out Spencer handed me a little plastic Disney bag with a box in it. I opened the box, and there was his grandma's ring. I was totally surprised. He kneeled down right in the midst of the departing people and proposed. I accepted, and we drove home that night to tell my parents.

Spencer and I moved in together. He was working at a law firm; I was working at the restaurant and still looking for a job. At the law school there was a career fair, and a legal aid program called "Put Something Back" was there. I decided if I couldn't find a job, I would at least volunteer. This gave me time to complete working my twelve steps.

I got a new sponsor, a caring woman named Ella. Ella led me deeper into the twelve steps. I was able to connect with people from my past and repair those relationships. I had begun to accept my sexual addiction and was able to abstain from self-abusive masturbation. I gave up cigarettes.

I also made a few very dear female friends who were in recovery too. We shared our stories and began to live and laugh. They began to reflect back to me a Jennifer I might someday be able to like—or even love.

CHAPTER 28

Then I got my first professional position; I was hired as a law librarian for the county. This was a great job because I could arrange to attend twelve-step meetings, and it did not require taking any cases home at night. I was still depressed and still hated myself, but I was unsure of why or what was festering. A friend suggested that I read the book *The Artist's Way* by Julia Cameron. I read it and followed its recommendation of writing three pages in a journal every morning. As I wrote day after day, I began to face my past.

At the milestone of two years sober, I still was not feeling all right. There was a woman in my home group named Diane, and the voice that had led me at various times in the past spoke to me again and told me that I needed to do a fifth step with her. The fifth step involves admitting "to our Higher Power, to ourselves, and to another human being the exact nature of our liabilities and our assets." I came to find out that Diane suffered from rape and abuse as a child, and we had a lot in common. She became the first person I really trusted with my entire story. I soon was united—through divine intervention, it seems to me—with a few other incest survivors who all shared their stories.

I was two years sober and something was wrong. I was married to a nice man. I had a fairly good job. I had worked the program of recovery. I had let go of all my anger from the alcoholism and made my amends for my behavior while drinking. So what was wrong? I was still having panic attacks. I was still angry. Something was wrong. I remembered something I had been told at some point, that I was only as sick as my secrets. I decided to trust Diane with one of my secrets.

I had never told anyone about my chronic masturbation problem. I told Diane. She looked at me and asked if I had ever been molested. I only told her at this point about the babysitter who had touched my sister and me. She told me that she had also been molested. She had experienced many years of recovery, and talking to her gave me hope. Diane had true light in her eyes. She loved herself.

"Maybe you need to stop beating yourself up with shame," she said. She told me that she thought I was very creative. She further explained that my masturbating was a very creative way to deal with my abuse and the confusing sexual feelings thrust upon me. She told me to get back into therapy. So I did.

CHAPTER 29

Around this time my uncle came down to visit and immediately started fighting with my mother. He told Papa that my mother was bad and was trying to turn Nana away from him. He was lying. Then Papa told Nana that Mommy was trying to do something hurtful. He was lying. Why was he lying? When I went back home to Miami with Spencer, I was confused. I started obsessing about this situation, worried about how it was affecting my mother.

I called Papa to ask him why he was lying about this. He started screaming. I responded in kind and started screaming at the top of my lungs, "Papa! It's me, Jennifer! Why are you doing this? Why are you lying?"

Suddenly, something snapped. It was as if my body and

mind were taken over by a powerful and sharp awareness. I hung up the phone. I looked around our apartment as if I were seeing it for the first time. The cabinets and table were from Nana and Papa's Cape Cod house. The dishes were the dishes we had always used there. Aunty Judy's big paintings hung on my wall. Suddenly, all these things from the past stood out as if in a spotlight, these things I had taken for granted ever since we had put them in place.

"Oh, my God," I thought. "Something's wrong. What is it? What happened?" I started breathing as if I were sobbing; I couldn't catch my breath. I crossed my arms in front of my stomach and starting moving back and forth. It all started coming back in a wave. Suddenly I was inside Nana and Papa's house, just as when I was a little girl. Memories crowded my mind, clear scenes of the abuse. It was as if I were back with Nana and Papa, in their house, surrounded by their things, helpless. I could see Papa's chair. The afghan. I remembered everything. The carpet. The wallpaper. The rooms. The kitchen. The frying pan.

Oh, no! Oh, no! It couldn't be! It couldn't be, I told myself. "Oh, no," I said out loud. "Papa loves me. He is good. He and Nana love me. They couldn't. They couldn't.

How could they? How could they? How could they?"

Slowly, gradually, the panicky feeling lifted. I felt weak and strong at the same time. I went to the phone and fumbled with it. I dialed their number again. When Nana answered, I said, "Nana, do you remember hitting me on Billings Street?"

"What?" she said.

"Do you remember hitting me on Billings Street?" I said, louder.

"What?"

"Hitting me on Billings Street!"

Instead of an answer, I heard Papa in the background. "Hang up the phone!" he screamed.

The next day Spencer received a message on the phone machine from my Aunt Judy, saying I was crazy and needed to be institutionalized.

CHAPTER 30

But, of course, all of it was true; all those scenes had taken place. Once the memories began to return, more and more of my past was restored to me. It was powerful, overwhelming at times. As I remembered what had happened, I would feel amazed that I could have suppressed these terrible events.

From then on, continuing for about two years, I went to see my therapist, Dr. Anne, every Saturday. Every Saturday I would tell her a new memory. She listened. She did not doubt me. She believed me. She encouraged me to slow down. To heal.

I talked to Diane about the memories, too. She would drive me around just to let me scream. I was so angry. Why? How? How could these things have happened? How could the memories have gotten lost?

It got worse. I remembered Hal and Elaine and everything they had done. The pictures were all there, in my mind. They had been there all along. They were surfacing, perhaps, because I was ready deal with them, because it was time to face them.

I told my parents. They believed me to the best of their ability. Daddy even went to counseling with me once. I wanted their support, but it didn't matter if they were having a hard time understanding and accepting. I was going to heal no matter what.

For the next two years I spoke with Diane every day. She helped me sort through my responses, helped me see which were authentic and which were not. She allowed me to get angry. When the truth about Hal and Elaine surfaced, she listened and did not judge me; she just loved me. She was and is a very dear friend. We drove and talked; I would sometimes scream with anger and pain. Sometimes it would get so bad that I wanted to jump out the window and die. Diane stayed calm and quietly reminded me what she said so often, that it would get better. She explained that the only way out is through.

With her help and Dr. Anne's help and the many books I read, I began to see that a part of me was frozen in time emotionally and that I had to feel all my feelings from my entire life up to this point to become whole, to be able to live authentically, to free myself from the past. With the feelings of anger and pain came a miracle. I truly began to feel joy again. I actually thought maybe I would sing again. Diane and the other women in our support group encouraged me.

Diane told me I had to start looking in the mirror and say "I love you," to myself. I couldn't do it. All I saw in the mirror was gross. I hated myself. She told me to try writing it down. Also it was suggested that I read two books that talk about affirmations, Louise Hay's *You Can Heal Your Life* and John Bradshaw's *Healing the Shame that Binds You.* I was told that it took 25,000 positive thoughts to erase one negative thought. I started the affirmations. I filled many journals. I began to notice that certain affirmations really worked, really made me feel better: "Jennifer, you are worthy" and "Jennifer, you are deserving."

In all the shame, I neglected to care for myself. I could go days without a shower. I liked baggy clothes that didn't touch my skin. If the clothes were too tight, I would instantly feel shame. Diane and my other friends encouraged me to care for myself, to buy nice things for myself. I did not feel worthy. Although one part of me was aware that I needed and deserved nice things, emotionally I kept myself trapped in a prison of self hate.

I owned two suits. One black and one navy blue. They were cheap and I alternated wearing them, the black one day and the navy blue the next. My friends told me to go shopping.

It was difficult. I did not feel like I deserved it. One day after work, at the urging of Diane and the others, I went to the store to buy some new suits. (I reminded myself that I worked full time and had to dress for my job as one way to make myself do this.) I bought a red one, a fuschia one, and a mint-green one. It was a small victory. One of my girlfriends took me to get my first pedicure and my first massage. (Letting another person, especially someone I did not know, touch me was very scary, very threatening.)

But with time my healing progressed, and I started to feel more comfortable in my own skin. I began to trust others. Little by little, the walls I felt between me and the rest of the world slowly began to disappear.

Dr. Anne recommended I read any book on incest and rape that I came across. One day I was in a bookstore and I picked up *Reach for the Rainbow* by Lynne D. Finney. The author is an incest survivor who had become an attorney and then a therapist. The book dealt with many of the things I was feeling. I felt comfort in reading the story of this survivor, and I learned an important truth: the journey to healing is a long one, but it is worth it. It is hard work. We are worth it.

Another book I read around this time was *Reclaiming Your Garden* by Karla McClaren. This book is a creative visualization and meditation book for survivors; through it, I learned how to go into my mind and claim my lost child who was stuck in a very dark place. With the help of this book, I created a beautiful and colorful garden for her to live in.

I read other books by survivors after these and felt some of the shame dissipate as I began to understand that, truly, I was not alone.

There is something strange that happens sometimes when someone comes into my life that I am sure is not safe. I instantly feel terrified and then I feel a physical reaction, a confusing sexual feeling. I am completely frozen and confused by this. I know inside that I cannot trust that person, but orgasm during my abuse created a sense that maybe my inner feeling was incorrect. It is a very confusing thing to be at war with your body.

Spencer was so supportive. He even bought me a punching bag and stayed with me while I punched and cried. There were periods of months when I could not be sexual. He always understood. One day he came home from the courthouse with a brochure for the VOICES conference, a conference for incest survivors. He encouraged me to go. It was amazing. I took a whole-day rage seminar and heard others' stories. I was not alone. I was okay.

The shame still ate away at me. I went to acupuncture every week and got massages regularly to help myself feel more comfortable in my body. I still looked in the mirror with hate. But inside I started to feel a small light growing.

I continued my morning journal pages, and decided that my women's group was a safe place to start singing. At one point we were all gathered around, and I decided to sing "Amazing Grace" for them. They were so kind. This was safe. This was good.

CHAPTER 31

Recovery from incest is a long process. I had built up so much anger and shame that it would take many years to begin to move past that pain, to knock down the wall I had built in order to survive. I was willing to do anything. I began work that will probably continue to some degree for the rest of my life. I read every single book I could find. In addition to therapy and meetings, I tried acupuncture, Reiki, and crystals meditation. Drum circles. Rage seminars. Conventions for incest survivors. Through all these experiences I was able to uncover and lessen some of the anger and shame I had built inside. My therapist tried to encourage me to take some medicine for the pain, but I chose not to. Instead, I would find myself with all the doors locked, trying not to jump off my balcony. I experienced all the pain and suicidal feelings of hopelessness I could handle. My husband and my friends helped me through.

As I continued to write in my journal, I began to recover various parts of my fragmented heart. I recovered my passion for music. With the help of some of my women friends, I began to sing again. I also rediscovered my passion for Judaism. The art of the cantor combines music and Judaism, and I was drawn to study to become a cantor. In another demonstration of what I see as divine intervention, when I called the orthodox seminary and was told by a rabbi—he seemed shocked at my request—that I could not study there, someone who heard him talking on the phone called out, "Wait!" and reminded the rabbi of an alternative. That was how I ended up taking private lessons and learned the traditional melodies for the service.

I drove an hour and a half once a week for the lessons, and it was on this drive that I began to hear the Shema. The Shema is part of every service and many Jews, upon awakening and when falling asleep, say the words of the Shema: Hear, Israel, the Lord is our God, the Lord is One.

Shema Yisrael Adonai Eloheynu
Adonai Echad

In the Torah, Moses uses the Shema to remind the Israelites of their God. In the car I heard the Hebrew voice say the Shema over and over almost as if someone were screaming at me to listen to it. When I returned home, I recorded what I heard and wrote my first musical piece. It was about a survivor of the Holocaust who had stopped hearing both the Shema and God because of anger.

I wrote a couple of other musicals this way. My teacher got the opportunity to lead a large congregation up north, and I got the opportunity to star in a brand-new musical being debuted in a small theater. I completed the musical run, but the hopes we had for its success were not realized. The failure of the production caused me to become depressed. I continued to journal, and the voice told me to start playing guitar. I was still working as a law librarian, and now I was taking guitar lessons once a week. I quickly picked up all of the chords on the guitar and began matching these chords to songs and poems I had written. Soon I started playing open-mike events. After a year of open mikes, I got my first paying gig. For four years I traveled around south Florida, even making a trip up to Nashville. I recorded and sold my own live CD. During this time I used my training as a cantor to perform a wedding ceremony and to try out for one of the seminaries in New York.

I spoke of my spiritual life and about abuse in my music. With every performance of every song, I found myself healing a little bit more. I could no longer tolerate working full time and traveling to perform, so I decided with my husband that I would take one year to do just music. I toured extensively and wrote. I did not find this way of life satisfying. I had thought that I wanted to perform for others—that God wanted me to do this—but something in my heart made it clear that this was not what I needed to do.

I continued to perform and got a part-time job working for a non-profit organization that helped ex-felons reenter society. While working at this job, I wrote my first one-woman show, "Sister Shameless." The entire show was a combination of my music and monologues about the shame I had felt and recovered from. I performed the show successfully in a couple of local venues.

At the same time I found myself drawn to the youth center at work. I decided to accept the position of director of the youth center, assisting young people—they were between sixteen and twenty-one and had felony records—in getting education and employment. Working at the center I came across many kids who had suffered just like I had, but who had expressed their shame and rage in different ways. I was able to teach anger management and behavior modification and mostly to love and to accept them for who they were. It was often painful, as when I saw many times what happened when suffering was greater than hope and a young person returned to the streets, unable to overcome the shame.

The abuse and addiction in my past had given me the experience that helped me understand what these other victims of abuse had gone through. During this time I also sponsored many women through the twelve steps of recovery. Most of the women that I worked with had also suffered from incest or rape and were struggling to shed the same shame that I was.

I became pregnant and gave birth to my beautiful son. This process was very confusing. I loved him, but I was terrified of being a parent. When my son was born I had a dream, and in the dream the archangel Gabriel came to me and showed me the Hebrew letters for Chai: Life with hearts bursting from its center. I woke up thinking over and over again that life was to be filled with love.

Recovering from abuse is a cyclical process; once again I found the goodness in my life, and doing so helped give me the strength to face some more pain. I would stare at my baby's beautiful face and feel awful inside, unworthy and hollow. I wanted to die. It turned out that I was suffering from post-partum depression. I went on medication for it, and immediately I began to feel better. (This was the same medication which my therapist had tried to get me to take many years ago, and in this instance, it was a lifesaver and also was an eye-opener.) I began to process my pain in a different way. Finally, I began to have love and compassion for myself and what I had experienced.

I stayed on the medication for almost two years and then was able to stop taking it. It truly provided a bridge for deeper healing, and I would use it again to help me process deep emotional pain.

CHAPTER 32

My husband changed law firms, and we had to move. It was a good move. We bought a beautiful home and created a good place for our son to grow and develop. More and more often, I found myself able to breathe freely.

I was soon to be ten years sober, and I still felt like I had some anger or pain inside me. The voice again spoke to me and told me to attend a codependency group. I did. I met a new sponsor and began to work the steps. This time was different. This time was kind and peaceful. I could see that I needed to forgive the abusers from my past, but I was having difficulty with this concept.

One day the voice told me to go into a local synagogue, one we had never attended. I walked in and knew I was home.

I found the same songs and people from my childhood. My family and I began to attend Shabbat services regularly. I lit the candles at home every Friday. It seemed to me that God spoke to me one morning and told me it was time to start cantoring again. The voice told me to walk into temple and go up to the pulpit in the middle of the day and sing the Kaddish. I did.

I called my rabbi and asked him if he would mind teaching me his service. He recorded a CD for me and gave it to me that night. Less than two weeks from that day, we were shocked to find out that he had been fired from our temple. Instead of reacting with anger, as I would have in the past, I found myself propelled to the pulpit. Soon I was leading services. I began reading the Torah and speaking to the congregation about my life. When I sang the Amidah in the temple for the first time, I was so happy that I thought my heart would explode with joy. God had saved me, and I was here to tell my people all about it. I assisted in the High Holy Day services and delivered a sermon to over 200 congregants. I was finding opportunities to tell more and more Jews about the loving God in our Torah.

An important part of my progress to this point happened

after our temple had decided to part ways with the rabbi and I volunteered to lead weekly Sabbath Services. As part of my leading, I was asked to read a personal comment on the Torah portion of the week. (The Torah is divided in fifty-two weeks, and each week we read one portion.)

At the time this request was made, I was watching Larry King one night and there was a Christian preacher named Joyce Meyer on. She was going public with the knowledge that she was an incest survivor and had suffered sexual abuse and rape. She had written a book that focused on using the Bible as part of the process of healing from abuse. This awoke many emotions inside of me. First, I was excited that another woman had exposed her own sexual abuse to the light. Next, I was curious as to how she used her faith to heal. Third, I was again experiencing the emotions of being somehow left out as a Jew and how this led to more shame. I decided after watching this program and subsequently reading Mrs. Meyer's book that I would use the opportunity of leading services to go through the Torah and find the healing messages throughout. I hoped to find a way to show Jewish women who were victims of abuse how they might use their faith to heal. I wanted to reach out my hand to them and demonstrate through my example that there are many ways to heal and that each one is equally valid.

So, I began to speak out.

Soon my husband and I joined the temple's board, and we began working to build up the congregation for a new rabbi. Also at the time I was accepted into a cantorial training institute set up for distance learning. I am thinking about entering that program as a way to help me continue my journey to serve God, even as I continue to heal from the wounds of my past.

CHAPTER 33

Forgiveness is tricky business. It must be done with impeccable timing and pure motives. Mainly, it should advance the healing of the one who is forgiving. One cannot forgive with the intention of receiving an apology from the wrongdoer or any sort of justice. After our son, Sawyer, was born I wanted to come to some sort of peace with Nana and Papa. I felt strange keeping them out of his life, and I felt very guilty. I felt compelled to find some sort of forgiveness for them. When Sawyer turned a year old, I sent Nana and Papa a photo album from his first year and a letter of what I thought then was forgiveness. In the letter I thanked them for the positive things they had done and stated that I forgave them for the abuse and harm. I thought that I was free now that I had done the forgiveness thing.

A few weeks later Nana and Papa sent back their own letter: they denied everything. I cried and became very angry. I could not believe that they could just deny everything. I had hoped my "forgiveness" letter would bring some remorse or validation from their side. They did not provide it.

So I sent another letter, detailing everything they had done and seemed to have forgotten. I held nothing back and included even the most gruesome of details. I have not heard from them since. I do realize now that with my original letters of forgiveness, I was trying to relieve the guilt I felt for exposing my family's secret. I was in no way trying to relieve myself of the pain of the past. Forgiveness is acceptance of the past and an ability to let it go. I now work forgiveness by loving myself and looking at all the positive things that have developed within me as a result of my abuse.

Something else we were pleased about when Spencer moved to his new job was that my parents had relocated to West Palm Beach and would be able to help with Sawyer. Another positive development at that time was that in our new community, I quickly found a recovery-support network and immediately became a member of a group and went to meetings at night when Spencer got home. The days were made up of "mommy things." Mommy things included household chores, music and gym class, and, of course, other mommies. I thought I was over all of my insecurity when I joined my first mommy group. Unfortunately, I didn't feel comfortable in this group. I felt that the women in the group were worried about money and clothes, and I was worried about recovery and staying well for Sawyer. The old shame of being different returned. Thoughts of the alcoholism, the incest, the rape all kept bubbling up. But they would pass, and eventually I found some women that offered what I needed. Most importantly, I learned boundaries. I began to understand that I did not have to let people get close to me and my son until I was ready. I did not have to like everyone. I just had to be kind.

After two years I really missed writing and performing. I placed Sawyer a couple of days a week for three hours each day in a drop-off gymnastics program. During this time I started working on a new one-woman show. I found a lovely local theater and produced a full run of the show. Spencer helped me compose all the music, and I played a few characters.

When you suffer from incest, you try as hard as you can to preserve the family and keep the family safe from the secret being exposed. All self-interest leaves, and natural instinct for this family preservation takes over. I've learned now that every panic attack I had was a sign that I was not being true to myself. I have to pay close attention to how I am feeling before I decide to do something.

I still instinctively get scared when my mother gets upset or angry. I remind myself that I am safe and that she can take care of herself. The funny thing is that I think this has made me a better mother. Whenever Sawyer spills something, I see how scared he gets and I make sure not to react in any way that would indicate that it is a big deal. It makes me more conscious of giving him the freedom to be the child and feel safe and protected.

Taking care of myself seems to still go against my grain. I try to remember to make regular dentist and doctor appointments, but sometimes I forget. I also try to eat healthy food and buy fresh flowers for my home.

Exercise is extremely important for me. It helps me stay in the present and in my body. My mind becomes quiet, and I don't think of anything but the moment. I turn on the wildest hip hop and climb on the machine and go to it.

CHAPTER 34

It was time to go back to work. I needed some income, as from a part-time job, and was unsure of what to do. I was sitting in a twelve-step meeting and the voice inside said maybe I should check out working at a local alcohol and drug treatment center. I forwarded my résumé and was hired almost immediately. I eventually ended up working most of my shifts in the women's unit there. (I am still working there now.) Almost every day, at least one of the women will come to me and share a part of her past. Every day I share with them a part of mine. Working there helps me realize how far I have come in my journey. When I share my story, I remind them to take it slow and give themselves time to heal.

It is sometimes hard for me to remember that I am a human "being" and not a human "doing." I like to keep busy to feel good about myself. I like to have ten careers and ten hobbies. It can make for a less-than-serene life. I try to remember that although I am a mother, a wife, a lawyer, a cantorial soloist, a writer, a singer, an actress, and a chemical-dependency support tech, my real job is to heal.

I forget that as a human being I have the right to choose, and I also have the right to change my mind. For so many years I did not live life fully, so I find myself trying all sorts of paths which interest me. I have to watch out, though, because my self-abuse reflex can cause me to feel locked into a single path with no right to change my mind. I will try something and then feel so guilty if I decide that it's not for me after all that I have trouble leaving that path.

I find myself sidetracked by all sorts of things. And, of course, I cannot do them halfway: I have to be the best. I can't just sing at temple: I have to be kosher and become ordained. I can't just sell Mary Kay: I have to get the pink car in the shortest time ever. I can't just work in the treatment center for extra money: I have to become a counselor and save every girl I can find.

Living in a state of high anxiety can be hard to let go of. Everything seems to be a big emergency and something to worry about. I use my time in the morning to pray and meditate. I am learning to let go of things and not have to control everything in my surroundings.

CHAPTER 35

Recently I was blessed with a new mentor in recovery, Nora. Nora, a licensed therapist, is a beautiful woman who has experienced fifty-plus years of recovery. She came into my life just when I thought I had no more growing to do.

I was wrong. I had never admitted to anyone that I thought it was my fault that I was raped and molested by Hal, Papa, and Elaine. I never voiced out loud my sense that if I hadn't been singing and dancing, Hal wouldn't have hurt me. I felt that Nora was safe to tell. I told her, and she said, "Dear, isn't that what little girls do, sing and dance around?" This simple statement opened a new door for me. I could see myself as a little girl, harmless and innocent. And I cried for that little girl.

Nora patiently talked with me on the phone, kindly speaking about what a lovely little girl I must have been and helped me come to finally understand why I felt so much guilt, shame, and fear every time I performed, why it felt like I was ready for a fight instead of a performance.

Now I am free to sing without fear and with joy.

After Nora's comment helped me to that breakthrough, I realized I had been uncomfortable around children for some time. I was angry with them. I never really understood why. I thought there must be something wrong with me. Now, finally, I could see that I had projected anger on them because I was angry with my little self. Once I realized that I was just an innocent child when I was victimized, I began to see all children differently. I became free to have true love and compassion for my young self and all little children.

I took Sawyer to the community pool where there are fountains for all the kids to jump and play in. I watched my son and the other children, and I kept repeating in my head, "Isn't this what children are supposed to do? Jump and play." There were little girls around eight or ten years old playing, and I pictured my little-girl self playing with them and I felt joy. I pictured Sawyer playing with a young me, and I giggled like a child. I began to see and understand how innocent and helpless children are. It made me have more love and compassion for myself for struggling alone the way I did. I am healing.

Nora told me to look in the mirror and say "Jennifer, you are a nice person, and I care about you deeply." I tried it, and it went fairly well. I did not have the old hate I used to have for my image in the mirror. I actually have started to really appreciate and care for that person reflected in the mirror.

All these years later—over a decade—since I first began to heal, I still have to remember to take time for four things: rage, grief, creativity, and self-love. For the rage I don't need to scream and yell or use the punching bag anymore. Instead, I find some good old-fashioned heavy metal and rock-and-roll and jump on the exercise machine. Rage in the Machine or Public Enemy are my recent favorites. For grief, I make sure to watch good sad movies and just cry throughout. (Although lately I don't have trouble crying, I seem to be crying every other day. This I know is good. It means that the healing is continuing and that I feel safe to let go.) When a memory or feeling resurfaces, I pay attention and let myself remember or experience the feeling, no matter how painful.

For creativity I write poetry, play music, and paint. Sometimes even coloring with Sawyer does the trick. For love of self, I meditate and pray. I also remember Nora's admonition; I look at myself in the mirror and say, "I love you." I keep myself surrounded by people and things that fill my spirit with joy. I take walks in nature and swim in the ocean. I listen to positive CDs and regularly attend my meetings of recovery. I express my sexuality in healthy and loving ways. I get massages, manicures, and fresh flowers. When I feel uncomfortable, I listen, listen to others and listen to my mind and heart.

Every day I wake up and pray that I will stay sane and sober; every morning I read inspirational meditations. Some mornings I write in my journal, and every day I say this to myself: "Jennifer, today is a new day. Anything can happen."

Gratitude has been an incredible tool for me. I have learned to look at the good things in my life and be thankful. When I first got sober and started to heal, my sponsor taught me to write a gratitude list every night. It was hard at first to see what was good in my life, so I wrote things like "I am thankful for my sobriety, my health, and the beautiful things in nature." It did not come easy, and some days I was just faking it. But I kept on, knowing as I'd learned in my twelve-step organizations that sometimes it's helpful to "fake it until you make it."

Now my gratitude list is so long I could say it for hours. At night I say my prayers; I include all the things I am grateful for that I can think of at that moment. It is all about changing my perspective from dark to light. Now most of the time I see from the perspective of light, see my life filled with sunshine and joy, my future with hope. No longer do I ruminate on the miseries I experienced or on how life handed me a raw deal. Now I can truly see how each thing has molded me and made me the strong and loving woman I am.

On a bad day, I might find myself getting a little annoyed over minor inconveniences, or I might realize I've neglected to shower or otherwise take care of myself. I have learned to laugh at this, to try to analyze what might be causing me to feel the way I'm feeling, and not to take myself too seriously. On a good day I do not think of the past at all, and I live freely and joyously in the present.

Truly, I mostly have good days. I am grateful for every day and for all my many blessings.

ACKNOWLEDGMENTS

Heart-exploding thanks to the following individuals without whom this book would not be possible: Donna, a most talented editor and caring friend; Spencer, my darling husband and biggest cheerleader; Sawyer, my sweet son and brightest light; my parents for your bravery and humility in walking this journey of healing with me; and my sister, for your support and trust.

To Gail, Elisabeth, Eva, Adrienne, Sue, Pam, Debbie, Delores, Whirly-Bird, Debbie Blais, Brenda, Martha, Barbara, Cathi, Mercy, Delilah, Andrea, Gay, Carlee, Melissa, Mara, Nilda, Jennifer, and countless other women whose listening ears and words have guided me.

To the following teachers for your actions and words, spoken or written: Lynne Finney, Julia Cameron, Debbie Ford, Bill Wilson, Melodie Beattie, Louise Hay, SARK, Karla MacClaren, John Bradshaw, Deepak Chopra, Bob Proctor, Earl Nightingale, Mary Summer Rain, Alice Sebold, Brian Weiss, Rosemary Altea, James Van Praagh, Sanaya Roman, Caroline Myss, Napolean Hill, Oprah Winfrey, Estelle Frankel, His Holiness Dalai Lama, Zora Neale Hurston, Maya Angelou, Emily Dickinson, Bruce Springsteen, Reb Zalman Schacter-Shalomi, and Joyce Meyer.

To the VOICES organization and Ariel Jordan for your brilliant rage seminar. For Denton Russell's revolutionary Vocal Teachings and Tapes. To Flash and the Wallflower Gallery. To Jim and the Edge Theater. To Zach and the staff of the Cuillo Center. To Cantor Aaron.

To Art, I miss you.

To Juan and the staff at Hanley Center, to John and the staff of Transition, Inc. To Bill and Centerpointe Research Institutes. To Mike Dooley for his *Notes from the Universe.* To Reb Zalman and Reb Marcia and the Jewish Renewal Movement and its resources and countless others whose works have inspired me.

A NOTE ON THE TYPE

The text in this book was set in ITC Galliard, designed by Matthew Carter (b. 1937).

www.ingramcontent.com/pod-product-compliance
Lightning Source LLC
LaVergne TN
LVHW090941080826
845145LV00003B/847

* 9 7 8 0 9 7 7 3 3 6 5 8 6 *